CULTIVATING YOUR CATECHISTS

How to Recruit, Encourage, and Retain Successful Catechists

JAYNE RAGASA-MONDOY

THE EFFECTIVE CATECHETICAL LEADER

Series Editor Joe Paprocki, DMin

LOYOLAPRESS.
A JESUIT MINISTRY
Chicago

LOYOLA PRESS.
A JESUIT MINISTRY

3441 N. Ashland Avenue
Chicago, Illinois 60657
(800) 621-1008
www.loyolapress.com

Cover art credit: Ann Triling/Hemera/Thinkstock.

ISBN-13: 978-0-8294-4530-5
ISBN-10: 0-8294-4530-7
Library of Congress Control Number: 2017936851

Printed in the United States of America.
17 18 19 20 21 22 23 24 25 26 27 Versa 10 9 8 7 6 5 4 3 2 1

Contents

Welcome to The Effective Catechetical Leader Series v

About This Book vi

1 More Than Volunteerism: The Vocation of the Catechist.............. 1

2 The Right Stuff: A Catechist's Role Description 15

3 Getting People to Say Yes: Strategies for Recruiting Catechists 25

4 Laying the Foundation: Formation and Training of Catechists 37

5 Cultural Diversity: Mining the Rich Cultures of Catechists 49

6 Care and Feeding: Ongoing Formation of Catechists 61

7 Doing It "By the Book": Supervision, Evaluation, and
   Record Keeping 71

8 It's Rarely Simple: Handling Difficult Situations 87

9 Retaining Catechists: Support, Collaboration,
   Affirmation, and Public Recognition 97

10 No One Is an Island: Building and Nurturing a
    Catechetical Community 111

About the Author 127

Welcome to The Effective Catechetical Leader Series

The Effective Catechetical Leader series provides skills, strategies, and approaches to ensure success for leaders of parish faith-formation programs. It will benefit anyone working with catechists, including Directors of Religious Education, pastors, diocesan directors, and catechetical training programs. Combining theory and practice, this series will

- provide practical instruction and printable resources;
- define the role of the catechetical leader and offer specific and practical strategies for leading, collaborating, and delegating;
- offer approaches for leading and catechizing in a more evangelizing way; and
- describe best practices for recruiting, training, and forming catechists; developing a vision for faith formation; forming an advisory board; planning and calendaring; networking with colleagues; selecting quality catechetical resources; handling the administrative aspects of the ministry; and identifying various groups to be catechized and approaches that meet the unique needs of those various groups.

Whether you are starting out as a catechetical leader or have been serving as one for many years, **The Effective Catechetical Leader** series will help you use every aspect of this ministry to proclaim the gospel and invite people to discipleship.

About This Book

This book of **The Effective Catechetical Leader** series focuses on nurturing the vocation of the catechist. The *General Directory for Catechesis* reminds us that "no methodology, no matter how well tested, can dispense with the person of the catechist in every phase of the catechetical process" (*GDC*, #156). As such, it is imperative that catechetical leaders do everything in their power to call quality candidates to the vocation of catechist, provide formation and training, and nurture their vocation every step of the way.

1

More Than Volunteerism: The Vocation of the Catechist

A friend of mine recounted an experience on a recent trip to Israel. Traveling through the arid countryside, his tour group paused to admire a section of verdant pasture. There, he observed two shepherds conversing with one another. As the shepherds spoke, their flocks of sheep merged together, forming a large, single flock. As he was pondering how the shepherds might identify their respective sheep, both shepherds called out in their own special voice. To my friend's astonishment, the sheep responded to what they knew to be a familiar and trusted call. They separated once again into two flocks and followed their shepherds.

As Christians, our vocation—literally a "call"—is from Jesus, the Good Shepherd. It is a call to holiness and a way of life in service to Him.

A Divine Call to Holiness

Many voices call out for our attention. Indeed, there are many laudable and noteworthy forms of volunteerism that organizations and communities depend upon. To serve as catechist, though, is to hear and respond to the Good Shepherd in a unique way by formally transmitting the faith to others. And one of the greatest responsibilities of the catechetical leader is to accompany the catechist on this journey.

As we seek out new catechists, we may find that many people seem overwhelmed by the prospect of following this divine call:

"Who, me? My faith is simple. I'm not a scholar of the Bible or of the *Catechism of the Catholic Church.*"

"There's so much to teach, I wouldn't know where to start!"

This hesitancy isn't surprising when we consider the depth and breadth of the Catholic Church and our desire to be true to her teachings.

The reality is, the vocation of catechists starts with a very simple act of faith. It starts when we say, "I believe," with a humble heart that says yes to living as a disciple of Jesus and to formally teaching others on a weekly basis to do the same. It is a desire to surround people of all ages with a community of believers who love, understand, and practice the faith. It is the willingness to share God's love story for us, one that unfolds every moment of our lives, touches us deeply, and influences every aspect of our lives. This simple, joyful vocation is what we are calling people to follow.

A Vocation Story

At the age of seven Mark decided that he wanted to become a musician. Singing hymns with the parish choir made him feel closer to God and his family. Mark's dad, an accomplished jazz pianist, played professionally in his younger days. Mark's mother, with her golden voice, would add beautiful melodies to his dad's deliciously satisfying tumble of improvisational tunes. The scene of his parents creating music together became etched in his mind—his dad seated at the piano in the living room, smiling as his fingers moved deftly across the keyboard; his mom, with a hand placed gently upon her husband's shoulder, vocalizing syncopated rhythms. They each possessed a God-given gift of music that was expressed uniquely but always in accompaniment with each other.

Mark recalled his dad saying that, while a classically trained musician, he loved playing improvisational jazz because it allowed his love for the music to overflow from the depths of his soul. He added that it was a good thing his wife accompanied him frequently. "When I get lost in the music, I can always find my way home, son. I just follow your mother's gorgeous voice."

Later in life as a successful musician himself, Mark finally understood why he felt called to his profession. It was not about his dad's skillful ability to read and improvise music or his mother's perfect pitch. It was not about an instrument or the applause they received from an appreciative audience. It was about the gifts from God that they received, nurtured, and shared. It was about the realization that in the accompaniment was creativity and a boundless expression of love for the music, but mostly for one another. It was about the security Mark felt as he witnessed their loving interaction that gave him the courage and desire to emulate them. He was convinced that God was a musician.

Mark's vocation—his calling—was born from love.

And so it is with the vocation of the catechist: God, who is love, transforms us. Jesus accompanies and nourishes us so that we may be creative and boundless in our expressions of love, and the power of the Holy Spirit gives us the strength to remain in his love. Our primary focus is not on how much we know (although that's important), the countless hours we spend preparing and teaching lessons (although they are appreciated), or the affirmation we receive from others (although that is, well, affirming!). The vocation of the catechist is first and foremost a call from Love to love.

Christ's Love Compels Us

The heart of the catechist receives the gift of the kerygma, and in turn offers it to others as a gift. What a little word: "gift"! The catechist is conscious of having received a gift, the gift of faith, and he or she then gives that gift in turn to others. This is something beautiful. We don't keep a percentage for ourselves! Whatever we receive, we give! This is not commerce! It is not a business! It is pure gift: a gift received and a gift given. And the catechist is right there, at the center of this exchange of gifts. That is the nature itself of the kerygma: it is a gift that generates mission, that compels us to go beyond ourselves. Saint Paul says that "the love of Christ compels us," but this "compels us" can also be translated as "possesses us." And so it is: love attracts us and sends us; it draws us in and gives us to others. This tension marks the beating of the heart of the Christian, especially the heart of the catechist. (Pope Francis, International Congress on Catechesis, September 2013, #2)

Pope Francis's words that the "love [of Christ] attracts and sends us" captures the essence of the catechist's vocation. We have received the gift of faith and are transformed by the gospel. In turn, Christ compels us to go out, encounter, accompany, and engage others in his name. Not only to those who believe, think, and act as we do but also to everyone we encounter.

Jeri's story stands in stark contrast to Mark's. Her parents bickered constantly between episodes of heavy silence. At her mother's insistence, the family attended Mass, but only on Christmas day, Easter Sunday, and the occasional Catholic wedding or funeral. Jeri was baptized Catholic and received first Penance and Eucharist, but her parents never consistently enrolled her in the parish faith-formation program and rarely spoke of their Catholic faith in the home.

The Scripture stories she did remember seemed foreign to her: the Holy Family, the Prodigal Son, the Good Shepherd. Where was the holiness, a loving father so quick to forgive, a parent who would notice when she seemed lost? When she turned fourteen, Jeri stopped going to Mass altogether. It just didn't make sense.

As evangelizing disciples, catechists are called to bring the Good News to others, especially to people like Jeri and her family. We seek the lost, welcome them home in a loving embrace, and help them to begin anew by treating them with compassionate mercy. This is a true testimony of Christian living and discipleship and a part of the vocation of the catechist.

In his homily at the 2016 Mass of the Holy Spirit at Catholic University in Washington, D.C., Cardinal Donald Wuerl offered a four-point description of behaviors for the evangelizing Christian that aptly applies to the vocation of the catechist. We are to go out, encounter, accompany, engage.

Go Out

Cardinal Wuerl stated that Pope Francis has urged us repeatedly "not to remain closed-in on ourselves, to remain focused on the affairs of the Church, but rather to reach out and meet people who should be with us and who are not." He continued: "I often find at the Easter Vigil, when I am speaking with those to be received into the Church or in the process leading up to their reception into the Church that many times when I asked what brought you to this point, the answer is very simply, 'Someone asked me, someone invited me.'"

As catechetical leaders, we are often preoccupied with the many operational aspects of our parish catechetical programs. This is quite understandable! It takes time and energy to call forth catechists, see to their ongoing faith formation and training, secure quality resources, hold parent meetings, plan retreats, and handle correspondence. Many parents of children who are registered in our programs are themselves in need of opportunities to be formed in faith. Indeed, there is much to be done. So, our challenge as catechetical leaders is never to lose sight of that personal touch that Cardinal Wuerl described.

The church exists to bring the life and love of Christ into the world, not just to our own parishioners who are registered in our programs. As a parish community, under the guidance of your pastor, consider the following questions that can help you foster and maintain this "go out" attitude that Pope Francis spoke of:

- Who is missing in our faith community? Where are they? Do we know persons who are in relationship with them? How can we, together, go out to them?

- Do we know our neighbors who live in close proximity to the parish? Do they receive invitations to open-house or hospitality events?

- How do we go out to parents who choose to have their children participate in sporting events on the weekend instead of attending Mass?

- How do we go out to the families of children with parents who are/have been imprisoned and can't get to Mass or the parish catechetical program?

- How do we go out to families of a child who has special learning, communication, or physical-access needs?

- How do we go out to families like the one in Jeri's story, who are struggling in their relationships?

For Reflection and Discussion: The vocation of the catechist includes going out to those beyond the parish. Consider the ways your parish ministry, including catechetical ministry to children and families, reaches out to people who do not come to Mass or those whom you see only on occasion. How can you improve on this?

Encounter

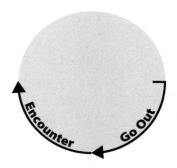

Here is how *Merriam-Webster's Dictionary* defines the word *encounter*:

a. To meet as an adversary or enemy
b. To engage in conflict with
c. To come upon face-to-face
d. To come upon or experience especially unexpectedly

A true encounter with the risen Jesus can transform lives. When we reach out to the greater community, however, we do face some real challenges, given the prophetic nature of the Gospel.

Yet Scripture reminds us that in each encounter we meet God face-to-face. The psalmist prayed,

> Hear, O Lord, when I cry aloud,
>> be gracious to me and answer me!
> "Come," my heart says, "seek his face!"
>> Your face, Lord, do I seek.
> Do not hide your face from me. *(Ps. 27:7–9)*

God has planted within us a desire to encounter his presence in every situation, even in times of adversity and conflict.

The catechist continually seeks opportunities to share this joyful message with others and to realize that God, who is love, is ever present in all our encounters with those he brings into our lives.

As you serve as a catechetical leader, consider discussing the following with catechists:

- We are surrounded by families who are in need of our prayers. How do we initiate an encounter with families who have recently suffered the loss of a loved one? Or lost a job? Or are facing a serious medical crisis? Have we offered to pray for and with these families?

- In times of joy, do we offer prayers of thanksgiving, modeling a grateful heart?

- When we meet with parents, do we teach them how to meditate upon Scripture? Do we create meaningful prayer services that include ways for them to participate?

- Do we share stories of the meaningful ways that God has touched our lives, and have we invited those we teach, and their parents, to do the same?

For Reflection and Discussion: What are some ways that your catechists reach out and encounter those in the wider community?

Accompany

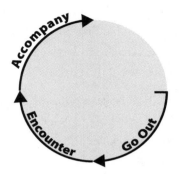

To accompany others is to walk alongside them as a companion on the journey of faith. We are grateful for the parents who attend Mass regularly with their child, who fully embrace their role as their child's primary catechist, and who enroll their child in the parish catechetical programs as an extension of the "domestic church," which is how the Catholic Church sees the family. Because we can relate to these families, accompanying them on the journey feels natural.

The reality is that we will often find ourselves walking alongside families and children who, like Jeri, still need the seed of faith that God has planted within them to be nurtured. When we are open, patient, and accepting and withhold harsh judgment of families, we create a sense of belonging—an important part of accompanying others. From there we are better able to help families look at the truth of their lives in light of Sacred Tradition and sacred Scripture.

This can be challenging. We sometimes bring preconceived attitudes and perspectives to our ministry about "those" children or families who do not behave or believe as we do. Gone unchecked, these attitudes will work against our goal to accompany people who are different from us. Instead, we are to take on the role of the father of the prodigal son, longing for their return and, when seeing them in the distance, running toward them to welcome them home.

We know we have truly abandoned ourselves to the ministry of accompanying others when the process seems as though we have removed our shoes and are standing on holy ground. In doing so, we will continually discover what a joy it is to accompany families!

To accompany others, we embrace the following notions:

- Special sensitivity is to be placed on the (pre-)evangelization process—the act of welcoming people and tending to their basic human needs (acceptance, security, etc.) as a means of preparing them to receive the Word of God.

- We are called to share with compassion and joy that Christ is present and at work in our lives and in all situations.

- All persons, all families, are holy, even (perhaps especially) in the chaos, messiness, or even apathy that is part of the human experience.

- In this "theology of presence," being silent together is a beautiful gift that we can offer one another, allowing God's message to fill our hearts. In the words often attributed to St. Francis of Assisi: "Preach the gospel at all times. When necessary, use words."

- There is no us/them. There is only *we*. Passing harsh judgment upon children and families who do not act or believe as we do is divisive and contrary to our divine calling to evangelize and catechize.

For Reflection and Discussion: The vocation of the catechist includes accompanying people of all ages on the journey of faith, especially in the messiness of life. What is your perception of families who do not attend Mass regularly or who do not act or believe as we do?

Engage

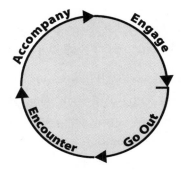

How would you describe an engaging person? A person who possesses positive attributes of engagement may be described as one who is a welcoming presence, is interesting, shares insights that are highly relatable, challenges you to rethink some of your own experiences, and thus helps place you on a holier path. It may be one whose corporal works of mercy inspire you. Or it may be as simple as one whose smile and personal style immediately build trust.

Effective engagement, however, helps us feel better about ourselves *and* is a call to action. The experience is so compelling that you are inspired to do the same. Positive engagement connects and challenges.

Cardinal Wuerl noted, "Not only do we attempt to walk with people, we want to engage them in the beauty and wonder of our Catholic faith. You and I believe that Christ is risen, that he walks with us and that we can touch him, reach him and be with him in the sacramental life of the Church. We need to have the confidence to say this when we are accompanying someone, so that we actually engage them in the life of the Church" (Homily, Mass of the Holy Spirit, September 8, 2016).

Thus, the vocation of the catechist includes

- Being attentive to our own prayer and sacramental life so that the beauty and wonder of the Catholic faith continually unfold for us.

- Authentically engaging others with an orientation toward Christ in word and sacrament.

- Embracing the challenge of the gospel, inspiring others to action and a deepened commitment to discipleship in Christ.

For Reflection and Discussion: The vocation of the catechist includes engagement. Describe some of the engaging behaviors exhibited by your catechists. How have they inspired others to action? What skills or faith-formation opportunities might they need to improve engagement?

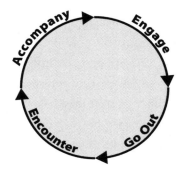

The vocation of the catechist is to go out, encounter, accompany, and engage, always confident that Christ is present and already at work in our lives and in the lives of those we serve. God not only accompanies us but is out there waiting for us. We can be assured that wherever we go, God is there first!

Summary: He Had to Go through Samaria

Now [Jesus] had to go through Samaria. So he came to a town in Samaria called Sychar, near the plot of ground Jacob had given to his son Joseph. Jacob's well was there, and Jesus, tired as he was from the journey, sat down by the well. It was about noon. When a Samaritan woman came to draw water, Jesus said to her, "Will you give me a drink?" (John 4:4–7, NIV)

The fact is, Jesus did *not* have to go through Samaria to get from Judea to Galilee. Most Jews of Jesus' time preferred to go around Samaria instead of passing through it. Jesus, however, chose to go through this territory where people considered "undesirable" lived. Jesus went forth, encountered, accompanied, and engaged the Samaritans there, beginning with the woman at the well.

As a catechetical leader, you are calling forth people who in turn are to call others to conversion. You are not just looking to fill slots with warm bodies; you are seeking people who are capable of responding to this extraordinary calling—this vocation—to serve as catechists.

Growing as a Catechetical Leader

As you prepare to call forth vocations to the catechetical ministry, take some time to reflect on your own vocation and how you have responded to God's call to go forth, to encounter, to accompany, and to engage.

Go to www.loyolapress.com/ECL to access the worksheet.

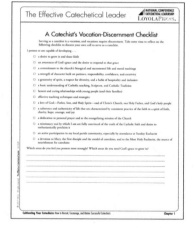

Suggested Action

Because serving as a catechist is a vocation, it makes sense that you begin your participation in calling forth vocations to this ministry by praying for the guidance of the Holy Spirit. Consider praying a novena: nine days of prayer (in imitation of the nine days the apostles and Mary remained in prayer between the ascension of Jesus and the coming of the Holy Spirit) using words such as the following each day:

Loving God, Creator of all things, you call us to be in relationship with you and others. Send forth your Holy Spirit to inspire faithful disciples of your Son to respond to the call to serve as catechists. May they accept the invitation to go forth, to encounter, to accompany, and to engage your people, bringing them into relationship with your Son, our Lord Jesus Christ. Amen.

For Further Consideration

The Catechist's Backpack. Joe Paprocki and Julianne Stanz (Chicago: Loyola Press, 2015).

The Catechist's Toolbox. Joe Paprocki and Doug Hall (Chicago: Loyola Press, 2007).

Consider Your Calling. Gordon T. Smith (Downers Grove, IL: InterVarsity Press, 2016).

The Volunteer Revolution: Unleashing the Power of Everybody. Bill Hybels (Grand Rapids, MI: Zondervan, 2004).

2

The Right Stuff: A Catechist's Role Description

In chapter 1 we talked about the vocation of the catechist as a call from Love to love. The role of the catechist is to walk the journey of faith with people of all ages, share the teachings of the Church, and help others recognize that Jesus is vibrantly alive, living among and within us. The *National Directory for Catechesis* tells us that "'within the whole process of evangelization, the aim of catechesis is to be the teaching and maturation stage'" with the "object of catechesis (as) communion with Jesus Christ" (*NDC*, #19–20).

You've Got to Hear This!

The Gospel of Luke describes an encounter with the risen Christ by two disciples on the road to Emmaus. While unrecognized at first, Jesus walked with them, taught them, and ate with them. Reflecting upon this experience, the disciples marveled: "Were not our hearts burning within us while he talked with us on the road and opened the Scriptures to us?" (Luke 24:32, NIV). The role of the catechist is patterned after Jesus' approach in this passage: accompanying, teaching, and sharing in the Eucharist.

Saint Luke continues, "They got up and returned at once to Jerusalem. There they found the Eleven and those with them, assembled together" (Luke 24:33, NIV). Filled with the realization of the risen Christ, the two disciples returned excitedly to Jerusalem. You can imagine them, their hands grasping the collars of some of the disciples, shouting, "You have got to hear this!" That's the spirit (pun intended) that is at the heart of the catechist's role.

Walk the Journey

Catechists often lament the limited time they have to spend with the young people in the parish catechetical programs. They may wonder, *What can one or two hours of contact time per week possibly accomplish?* First, we must help our catechists to realize that the time they spend with their students is always valuable, and second, remind them that they do this for the noblest of reasons—to help their students come to know the Person of Jesus Christ more deeply.

The longing we have for more time together with young people in our classes comes from a sacred source: God has planted within us the desire to spend our entire lives in search of ways to know, love, and serve him well. This is the journey of faith: it is not limited to weekly catechetical sessions; it is literally a lifetime adventure!

For catechists to walk this journey with those they teach and their families is to accompany them through life's natural progression and grow together in understanding God, the world, and ourselves. This quest transcends the classroom into life itself, as catechists inquire about the interests and activities of their learners, celebrate milestones such as birthdays, baptism anniversaries, and graduations, and offer to pray with and for them in times of sorrow. The time that catechists do spend in the classroom, then, becomes just one of many encounters they share as companions on the journey.

For Reflection and Discussion: In what ways do your parish catechists walk with students and their families outside the classroom?

Teach

Once catechists set out on this journey of faith with those they teach and their families, they may ask, "How, then, are we to teach?" As catechetical leaders, we can help catechists by inviting them to consider Jesus, the master teacher. In the story of the disciples on the road to Emmaus, Jesus begins with a question (the Socratic method) and allows the disciples to state their fears and doubts. He knew that they were confused about his Passion, death, and Resurrection and that they sought to make sense of what they were experiencing. In his great love for them Jesus placed himself on their path, listened patiently, and moved them past their fears as he "opened the Scriptures" (Luke 24:32, NIV).

Jesus was keenly focused on the disciples' learning experience. He connected the content of his message to their lived experience and asked clarifying questions. His words burned in their hearts, but Jesus knew that they needed more, so he lingered with them, finally sharing in a communal ritual that led them to an *aha!* moment. In other words, they achieved the primary learning objective for the day: the realization that Jesus is alive! "He had been made known to them in the breaking of the bread" (Luke 24:35).

Effective teaching requires more than imparting knowledge. Catechists are called to place emphasis on the learner and to be sure that their approach is learning-focused, engaging, and creative. Catechists should present content in a way that is relatable and inviting so learners can make connections, draw their own conclusions, and achieve their own *aha!* moments. The great thing about this process is that it doesn't stop there. A learner inspired by an encounter with Jesus can't help but joyfully share the experience with others: to declare with confidence that Christ is alive and to follow him. This action, called evangelization, is the primary learning objective for the catechist and, in particular, for the catechetical leader.

For Reflection and Discussion: Are your catechists' lesson objectives learning-focused? How do catechists incorporate the lived experiences of learners and their families into their lessons?

Christ Is Alive!

We as catechists are agents of evangelization. The realization that Christ is alive fills our hearts with a joy that overflows into the world, a continuous action of receiving from God and giving to others.

In his September 2013 address to the International Congress on Catechesis, Pope Francis taught that "the heart of the catechist always beats with this systolic and diastolic movement: union with Christ—encounter with others. Both of these: I am one with Jesus and I go forth to encounter others. If one of these movements is missing, the heart no longer beats, it can no longer live."

Let's examine Pope Francis's words.

- In baptism, we receive and accept God's loving invitation to be a member of the Christian community. The grace we receive in baptism is pure gift, given freely to strengthen our faith and to fuel a desire to be of service to others in the name of Christ. We receive and give: systolic and diastolic.
- At Mass, we receive Jesus in word and sacrament. He is alive in us and sends us forth into the world to be his disciples, modeling all that he has taught us. We receive and give: systolic and diastolic.

Those called to catechetical ministry mimic this heartbeat: the joy of the risen Christ that fills the heart is shared at each encounter with those they teach and their families.

For Reflection and Discussion: As a catechetical leader, what opportunities do you provide that allow your catechists to reflect upon and share their experiences with the risen Christ?

The Roles of the Parish Catechetical Leader and the Catechist

Now that we've examined the catechist's role through the lens of Scripture, let's consider how the roles of the parish catechetical leader and parish catechist help to form balance and cohesion in ministry. By baptism, all Christians are called to holiness. All have a role in the ministry of catechesis. However, those involved in the parish catechetical ministries participate in this responsibility in a more formal and visible way, and it makes sense to have a clear understanding of duties and expectations. In the *National Directory for Catechesis*, the bishops of the United States provide clear scopes of responsibilities.

It is important to note that these roles do not replace that of the parent, who is the first and most influential catechist in the life of a child. Indeed, parish catechetical programs are to assist parents in their holy responsibility of forming their child in faith. The role of parents as catechists of their children is explored in detail in books 5 and 6 of this series.

The Role of the Parish Catechetical Leader

Under the direction of the pastor, the catechetical leader is tasked with the following responsibilities:

- Overall direction of the parish catechetical programs for adults, youth, and children
- Planning, implementation, and evaluation of the parish catechetical program
- Recruitment, formation, ongoing development, and evaluation of catechists
- Implementation of diocesan parish catechetical policies and guidelines, including the areas of catechist certification and supervision, and administrative policies related to negligence,

sexual abuse, sexual harassment, and the safety and protection of minors

- Collaboration with the pastor, other parish ministers, and appropriate committees, boards, and councils
- Assistance in liturgical planning
- Attention to his or her own personal, spiritual, and professional development

The Role of the Catechist

- A love of God—Father, Son, and Holy Spirit—and of Christ's Church, our Holy Father, and God's holy people
- A coherence and authenticity of life that is characterized by his or her consistent practice of the faith in a spirit of faith, charity, hope, courage, and joy
- Personal prayer and dedication to the evangelizing mission of the Church
- A missionary zeal by which he or she is fully convinced of the truth of the Catholic faith and enthusiastically proclaims it
- Active participation in his or her local parish community, especially by attendance at Sunday Eucharist
- A devotion to Mary, the first disciple and the model of catechists, and to the Most Holy Eucharist, the source of nourishment for catechists

(*NDC*, #54)

This Heroic Task

While the role of a catechist is not rocket science, neither is it a role that can be filled by just anyone. Those called to serve as catechists must have specific skills and qualities to be able to effectively engage in this heroic task. In his book *The Catechist's Toolbox*, Joe Paprocki provides a summary of the qualities, knowledge, and skills of the catechist:

Qualities of an Effective Catechist

- A desire to grow in and share faith
- An awareness of God's grace and the desire to respond to that grace
- A commitment to the church's liturgical and sacramental life and moral teachings
- A strength of character built on patience, responsibility, confidence, and creativity
- A generosity of spirit, a respect for diversity, and a habit of hospitality and inclusion

Knowledge and Skills of a Catechist

- A basic understanding of Catholic teaching, Scripture, and Catholic tradition
- Honest and caring relationships with young people and their families
- Effective teaching techniques and strategies (Joe Paprocki, *The Catechist's Toolbox* [Chicago: Loyola Press, 2007], 5)

Articulating a specific role description for catechists will be of great assistance when calling forth catechists to serve in this noble and heroic ministry. What do we mean by "heroic"? Today, we describe people as heroic when they go out of their way to perform a service above and beyond the call of duty. While this is indeed true of catechists, there is another level of meaning to the word *heroic* that we can find in the tradition of the Jesuits, founded by Saint Ignatius of Loyola. It is common among the Jesuits to strive to make their work heroic, meaning that they are called to "aim high" and to offer nothing less than the highest quality and a desire to excel. To call someone to serve as a catechist is indeed heroic!

Summary: Jesus Sends Out the Seventy-Two

After this the Lord appointed seventy-two others and sent them two by two ahead of him to every town and place where he was about to go. He told them, "The harvest is plentiful, but the workers are few. Ask the Lord of the harvest, therefore, to send out workers into his harvest field. Go! I am sending you out like lambs among wolves. Do not take a purse or bag or sandals; and do not greet anyone on the road." (Luke 10:1–4, NIV)

In chapter 10 of Luke's Gospel, Jesus provides a role description of sorts for the seventy-two disciples whom he sends forth to proclaim the kingdom of God to others. People need to know what is expected of them when they are sent forth to perform a task. In a similar way, we need to articulate specific and reasonable expectations for those we are calling to serve as catechists. As a catechetical leader, you might find it very effective and helpful to publish a role description for catechists that identifies several basic expectations in the areas of knowledge and skills, along with responsibilities, to assist those who are discerning the call to this heroic ministry.

Growing as a Catechetical Leader

Have you ever thought of your own catechetical ministry as "heroic"? If not, you should! Be sure to take some time to reflect on how, in your ministry, you aim high and strive to offer nothing less than the highest quality and a desire to excel.

Go to www.loyolapress.com/ECL to access the worksheet.

Suggested Action

As you begin to identify prospects for the role of catechist, think of the most effective teachers you had. Identify several qualities and skills they possessed that you would like to see in the people you call forth to serve as catechists.

For Further Consideration

The Catechist's Companion. Cullen Schippe (New York: McGraw Hill, 1998).

Catechist 101. Carole M. Eipers (New London, CT: Twenty-Third Publications, 2014).

Heroic Leadership. Chris Lowney (Chicago: Loyola Press, 2005).

The Role of the Catechist. Cullen Schippe and Sr. Angela Ann Zukowski, from the Called to Be a Catechist series (New London, CT: Twenty-Third Publications, 2016).

3

Getting People to Say Yes: Strategies for Recruiting Catechists

"If you want to get something done, ask a busy person." This saying is a popular yet paradoxical idea. A person who is very busy often has a reputation for being reliable, capable, and open to serving others. Faced with the real challenge of seeking volunteer catechists, particularly when the need arises at the last minute, it is understandable to turn to those who are already actively involved in the parish. But these last-ditch efforts can be minimized when we take a more strategic approach to recruiting catechists.

A Call to Mission and Witness

Think of a strategy as a set of guiding principles to help you achieve a goal. Effective catechetical leaders base their strategy of recruiting on the belief that all who are baptized and confirmed are called to carry out the church's mission to give witness to Jesus. In addition, they know that the ministry of catechesis helps the faithful to relate and respond to this call.

Chrissy shares her story.

While saying good-bye to fellow parishioners after Sunday Mass, I peered back into the church and saw the parish catechetical leader kneeling in prayer before the statue of the Blessed Mother. She appeared serene, a gentle smile on her face. *Wow,* I thought. *Something wonderful must have happened in her life.* Making her way out of the church a few minutes later, she looked at me and said, "I had a great conversation with Mother Mary. Our faith-formation program starts in two weeks, and I told her that I need four more catechists. She reminded me that her Son's strategy didn't include a pulpit or bulletin announcement. He simply stated, 'Come, follow me.' I was reminded that it's all in the relationship and personal invitation to Christ, not about getting people to support a program."

Her eyes met mine as she continued, "With your full-time job and busy family life, I realize that asking you to volunteer your time is asking a lot. But I've witnessed your children grow up in faith since the time of their baptism. We need parents like you who can witness to Christian life and encourage others to do the same. You already have what it takes, and I promise that I will help you every step of the way. Will you help lead others to Christ?" And that's how I became a parish catechist.

Upon examining this story, we see several catechetical principles that appear to guide this conversation to its successful outcome. The leader believes that an invitation to catechetical ministry must

1. be centered in Christ
2. be an experience of evangelization and inculcation that touches the heart
3. stand at the crossroads of faith and life, sanctifying the human experience
4. include an assurance of accompaniment and skill development
5. be personal and joyful

Of course, each of us would have a unique way of wrapping our own story around these guiding principles. And whether you follow these or outline your own, formulating and applying a set of principles to your style of recruiting is a skill that takes practice and requires reflection and prayer to blossom. But that's the beauty of it! Drawing upon our own call and response to catechize, we become better at inviting others to do the same.

Recruiting Steps

There are practical strategies for calling people to serve as catechists. Meet with your pastor, who is the chief catechist and shepherd of the parish, as well as with the pastoral leadership team to consider and implement the following steps.

Think Stewardship

While it's tempting for a catechetical leader to focus solely on recruiting catechists to fill slots in the catechetical program, it is more appropriate to approach this task with the overall vision to be faithful stewards of the gospel. We're all familiar with parish stewardship: offering our time, talent, and treasure to build the kingdom of God. It's not about money but about a way of life. In their pastoral letter *Stewardship: A Disciple's Response*, the United States Conference of Catholic Bishops (USCCB) teach us that stewards "receive God's gifts gratefully, cultivate them responsibly, share them lovingly in justice with others, and return them with increase to the Lord."

Recruiting catechists is a natural extension of the overall vision of your parish stewardship plan. Start by raising awareness of the valuable gifts that the ministry brings to the parish. Share stories about children and families growing in faith. Ask catechists to share their stories about how their lives have been changed by cultivating and sharing their gifts.

In his preface to the pastoral letter, Bishop Sylvester D. Ryan, chairman of the ad hoc Committee on Stewardship, writes:

> Discipleship requires the surrender of ourselves through grace and choice to Jesus Christ: "Mature disciples make a conscious, firm decision, carried out in action, to be followers of Jesus Christ no matter the cost to themselves." A disciple is both a learner and a companion of Jesus Christ, as well as one open to the movement of the Holy Spirit towards a gracious generosity of heart. The authentic disciple regards all he or she is and possesses as gifts and blessings and realizes the need to share those gifts and blessings with others for the sake of the kingdom of God. (*Stewardship: A Disciple's Response: A Pastoral Letter on Stewardship*, USCCB, 1996)

Create (or Revisit) Roles and Responsibilities

With the overall vision for the catechetical program and a basic understanding of the needs of the parish in mind, state in writing the roles and responsibilities for your volunteers. A position description and catechist handbook are helpful recruitment tools because they give potential volunteers a basic understanding of what they're (hopefully) agreeing to. Refer to chapter 2 for specifics on the role of the catechist.

The preferred method of distribution is to personally hand, mail, or send electronically the role description to a potential volunteer while also making it available on the parish or religious-education Web site. Personalize the invitation by including a description of the qualities you see in that person and why you believe he or she would be a good fit with those being served. Remember, you are inviting others to discipleship in service to Christ, not to a program. Be sure to also follow up within the week.

Build a Team

If you are the only one doing the inviting, you likely have discovered that there are only so many individuals you can reach. If this is the case for you, it's time to do yourself a favor and start building a team of "inviters" who understand the program and are enthusiastic about it. While some may have larger-than-life personalities and others a quieter centeredness about them, your team should be composed of spirit-led individuals who

- listen well and identify in others gifts that are appropriate to catechetical ministry
- relate well to others and are easy to approach
- are involved in and understand the various roles within the ministry, such as lead catechist, aides, special programs (e.g., family retreats, prayer services), administrative or hospitality assistant, etc.
- enjoy inviting others to volunteer and don't take no as a personal affront
- represent your parish population in terms of age group (generation), ethnicity, etc.

Your joint task is to be "fishers of women and men." The last time I checked, it is rare for a fish to jump into a boat solely because people in the boat announced that they needed a fish! While announcements from the pulpit, church bulletin, or Web site are helpful, too often we rely solely on them. Then we don't understand why people are not immediately jumping into our program "boat." While you can continue to use these classic forms to recruit catechists, it is more beneficial and effective to have a team focused on building relationships that, over time, will present opportunities for a personal invitation to ministry.

Finally, decide which members of the team will be present at parish liturgical celebrations, community gatherings, outreach efforts, etc. Their (and your) presence increases the visibility of the program and gives witness to what it means to be a Christian disciple, evangelizer, and catechist.

For more ideas on how to attract potential catechists, go to http://catechistsjourney.loyolapress.com/ thinking-of-becoming-a-catechist/.

Identify Potential Pools of Candidates

Rather than just throwing out a net to see what you catch, it is much wiser to identify some target audiences or pools of potential candidates whom you can invite to serve as catechists. Consider the following sources:

- parents of children enrolled in the faith-formation program
- catechist aides
- retired parishioners
- RCIA neophytes (Caution: Avoid "pouncing" on neophytes immediately after the Easter Vigil! Give them some breathing space so as not to overwhelm them.)
- parishioners actively engaged in adult faith formation
- parishioners participating in lay-ministry formation programs
- members of the parish pastoral council (especially the education commission)
- professional teachers (public school and Catholic school)
- former catechists
- referrals from the pastoral staff
- recommendations from current catechists

Tap into the Reasons That Motivate People to Volunteer

As you call forth vocations to catechesis, it's good to know why people volunteer in the first place. Understanding why people volunteer makes it easier to identify and invite people to volunteer. Research shows that people volunteer for the following reasons:

- Achievement—to learn new skills, accomplish something worthwhile, increase self-esteem
- Challenge—to stretch themselves, discover gifts and talents
- Creativity—to express themselves creatively
- Independence—to undertake a task "on their own" (separate from spouse or family)
- Leadership—to develop personal leadership ability
- Recognition—to accomplish something that will reflect positively (to polish their résumé, etc.)
- Self-expression—to articulate and pass on strongly held beliefs
- Service—to be of service to others, to "give back"
- Socialization—to make new friends

Research also shows that women volunteer more than men, and the age group most willing to volunteer is between 35 and 44.

Create an Inviting, Pastoral Environment

Imagine walking into a retail store. In one corner you notice a customer attempting to get assistance from a salesperson who is busily stocking shelves. This salesperson finally notices the customer, heaves a heavy sigh, and utters a perfunctory and unsmiling, "Can I help you?" What would be your impression of that salesperson and the company he or she represents? No doubt you would think that the company and its employees are not very inviting or welcoming.

Catechetical leaders who are successful recruiters are mindful of the importance of creating an inviting and pastoral environment, often asking themselves the following questions:

- When people visit our catechetical program, what are their first impressions?
- Are there friendly exchanges among catechists, parents, and children?
- Do the learners seem engaged and happy to be there? Do parents share stories of how, in partnership with the parish catechetical program, their entire family is growing in faith?
- Do parishioners regularly hear about ways that children and families grow in faith through the program?
- Is the program regularly featured in a positive light in the diocesan newspaper, parish Web site, bulletin, and other forms of communication?

The bottom line is, a vibrant and welcoming environment attracts others to the ministry.

Create a Variety of Opportunities for Involvement

A popular strategy among professional recruiters is to "leave seats empty." By this they mean that it is better to leave a position empty than to fill it with a person who is unsuitable for the role. When someone turns out not to be suited to the role of catechist, rather than turn the person away, offer him or her another opportunity to be of service in ways appropriate to his or her gifts and talents. Perhaps, over time, those individuals may develop into catechists after all! Here are some examples of alternate ways of serving the catechetical program.

- Persons who are enthusiastic but untrained may be assigned to a mentor catechist until they complete diocesan certification requirements.

- Persons who are reluctant to be lead catechists may be assigned as aides.

- Persons who want to help but are reluctant to work with children may be invited to hold catechetical sessions with parents to help strengthen the domestic church or to assist with administrative duties.

- Persons who are unable to make a weekly commitment may be asked to assist with the occasional retreat or prayer service or coordinate a short-term special program (such as Catholic Relief Services' Operation Rice Bowl during Lent).

- Persons who are non-native speakers may help with interpretation/communication to children/parents.

- Persons who want to help but are not necessarily eager to interact one-on-one may be asked to assist with office/clerical help, parking-lot duty, hall monitoring, or other ways of ensuring the program runs smoothly.

Each of these practices helps to match program needs with appropriate volunteer gifts, fostering meaningful involvement, and also builds a pool of potential catechists.

Recruit Proactively and Continually

Recruitment is most successful when it is proactive and ongoing. Catechetical leaders prayerfully and continually seek to build relationships. They attend parish events and celebrations to develop a real appreciation for the diversity of parish life. They continually develop friendships in the community, especially with parents whose children are or have been enrolled in the catechetical program. And leaders find ways to keep sharing with others the meaningful stories about how serving as a catechist helps people grow deeper in their walk with Christ, and how it touches and influences the lives of families. Through these connections, they continually discover and establish

relationships with persons who are discerning a vocation to catechetical ministry.

In *Co-Workers in the Vineyard of the Lord,* the bishops of the United
States offer this reflection: "Among the baptized, all of whom are called
to serve the mission of the Church, some experience a further specific
call to lay ecclesial ministry. The call may come in a dramatic moment.
More often, it comes over time, as the person grows—within the community of faith—in love for God and a desire to do his will. One
begins to consider that the graces received could now be put in service
to the Church. A period of discernment begins" (29).

As you and your catechists continually invite new people to participate in catechetical ministry, the pool of potential volunteers will grow
deeper.

Finally: Treat Volunteers Well!

As volunteers step forward, treat them as the beloved members of a
family they are—members of the Body of Christ. Take care always to
be kind, considerate, and compassionate. If conflict arises, maintain
your composure; avoid making hurtful remarks or engaging in impulsive acts. A catechetical leader once admitted to me that in anger he
impulsively threw a perfectly good textbook out of a window—in the
presence of a class of fifth-graders—upon learning that their catechist
was using an older text and not the one currently assigned to the class.
The catechist quit that day. The following week, half of his catechists
followed suit. It took a month for him to make amends and for most,
but not all, of his catechists to return. Chapter 8 will explore healthy
ways to handle difficult situations.

Express your appreciation for what your volunteers are doing and
how their presence makes a difference in and to the church. People
volunteer because they want to make a difference in a meaningful way.
They stay because they feel cared for and appreciated.

Summary: Come and See

The next day John again was standing with two of his disciples, and as he watched Jesus walk by, he exclaimed, "Look, here is the Lamb of God!" The two disciples heard him say this, and they followed Jesus. When Jesus turned and saw them following, he said to them, "What are you looking for?" They said, "Rabbi (which translated means Teacher), where are you staying?" He said, "Come and see." (John 1:35–39)

Jesus did not put up posters or distribute literature inviting people to follow him; he used the personal approach. He asked people what they were looking for, and then he invited them to follow him and to discover what they were looking for. In your role as a catechetical leader, one of your highest priorities is recruiting—calling forth—catechists. While it is important to have literature to support your recruitment efforts, the most effective way to invite people to discern whether they have a vocation as a catechist is through the personal touch. Be sure to identify people's gifts, assemble a team to assist you, identify a pool of potential candidates, tap into the reasons people are motivated to volunteer, create an inviting environment, recruit proactively and continuously, and treat your current volunteers well!

Growing as a Catechetical Leader

It's important for us to have role models. In the church we are blessed to have the saints, who are examples for us. Saints Damien and Marianne are models par excellence of selfless volunteerism. Research their stories and reflect on ways that you walk in the footsteps of the saints, offering your life in service to God by serving his people. To find the stories of Saints Damien and Marianne, visit http://catholichawaii.org/ catholic-essentials/scripture-tradition/saints/saint-marianne/.
Go to www.loyolapress.com/ECL to access the worksheet.

Suggested Action

A good way to get into the minds and hearts of potential catechists is to ask your current catechists how they received the call to serve as catechists and what motivates them to participate in this ministry. Invite a group of your catechists to an informal gathering where you can pick their brains and their hearts.

For Further Consideration

Connect: How to Double Your Number of Volunteers. Nelson Searcy with Jennifer Dykes Henson (Grand Rapids, MI: Baker Books, 2012).

101 Strategies for Recruiting Success. Christopher W. Pritchard (New York: AMACOM, 2007).

Through the Year with the DRE. Gail Thomas McKenna (Mahwah, NJ: Paulist Press, 1987).

4

Laying the Foundation: Formation and Training of Catechists

Most new catechists have a deep love for the Church, her children, and their families. They also may approach the start of their ministry with great trepidation, as most of them are not professional teachers. Recognizing this reality, most dioceses require catechists to engage in a process of formation that leads to various levels of recognition and/ or certification. This is not simply a way for catechists to complete requirements or jump through hoops. Rather, leading a catechist to certification and beyond is one of the most powerful ways that a catechetical leader can bring prestige to the vocation of the catechist and prepare certain individuals to move into leadership roles themselves.

With the many hours already committed to parish ministry, leaders may feel reluctant to ask new catechists to complete the certification process. But think of it this way: through ongoing formation, catechists will improve their ability to evangelize, will come to know Christ more intimately, and will learn to teach as he did.

Christopher's Story

Christopher came bounding toward me with a huge grin on his face. "I'm so excited. I just completed all the requirements of the catechist certification program!" I congratulated him on his significant achievement. After all, he held a full-time job, was involved in parish ministry, and had a healthy social life. It took a great deal of encouragement, support, and commitment to complete the requirements of the rigorous program.

"So, Chris, have you been able to put your certification to good use?"

"Yes, I've been writing lessons that I plan to deliver as a catechist for my parish. I want to tell them all about Jesus!"

"That's great! There are a lot of ways we can tell others about Jesus. What do you have in mind?"

"Well, I can use stories, teach them how to pray, ask them about what is happening in their lives and how they can form themselves more closely to Christ. I can remind them that they encounter Jesus in a special way in the sacraments, especially in reconciliation and Eucharist, and to participate in the sacraments regularly, especially with their parents."

"And . . . ?"

"And I can tell my students about Jesus by treating others with dignity and respect, especially those who are the most vulnerable."

"What you're doing, then, is not only telling your students about Jesus, you're helping them to encounter him. You're also describing what Saint Pope John Paul II envisioned when he said that we are to preach the unchanging truth with 'new ardor, new methods and new expression.'"

"I never thought of it that way. It makes me want to continue learning about the Catholic faith."

This catechetical leader both encouraged and assisted Christopher to capture the richness of the ministry. In many ways, Christopher exemplifies what Pope Francis desires for the catechist:

The first thing for a disciple is to be with the Master, to listen to him and to learn from him. This is always true, and it is true at every moment of our lives. I remember, in the diocese, the other diocese I had first, how I would often see catechists finish their training courses and say: "I have the title of catechist!" This means nothing, you have nothing, you took a little journey. What good will it do you? But one thing is true. Being a catechist is not a title, it is an attitude: abiding with him, and it lasts for a lifetime! It means abiding in the Lord's presence and letting ourselves be led by him. (Pope Francis, International Congress on Catechesis, September 27, 2013)

The Absolute Priority of Catechist Formation

Just how important is catechist formation? The *General Directory for Catechesis* states: "Diocesan pastoral programmes must give absolute priority to the *formation of lay catechists*" (*GDC*, #234). In the *National Directory for Catechesis*, they outline a holistic approach:

The definitive aim of catechesis is to put people not only in touch but in communion, in intimacy, with Jesus Christ. . . . Jesus formed his disciples by making known to them the various dimensions of the Kingdom of God. He entrusted to them "the mysteries of the kingdom of heaven"; he taught them how to pray; he opened his "meek and humble heart" to them and he sent them "ahead of him in pairs to every town and place he intended to visit." The fundamental task of catechesis is to achieve this same objective: the formation of disciples of Jesus Christ. Jesus instructed his disciples; he prayed with them; he showed them how to live; and he gave them his mission. (*NDC*, #19B, 20)

The NDC summarizes the objectives of catechesis in the Six Tasks of Catechesis:

1. **Catechesis promotes knowledge of the faith.** Catechists are called to proclaim the gospel with joy so that those they teach, inspired by the Holy Spirit, will desire to know more about

Christ. They are to teach that God reveals himself in sacred Scripture and Sacred Tradition, and they are called to help others to know and better understand the Creed and the basic doctrines of the Church.

2. **Catechesis promotes a knowledge of the meaning of the liturgy and the sacraments.** Catechists are called to show Christ as present in the sacraments, inviting those they teach to experience him intimately in liturgical celebrations, especially the Eucharist. Catechists are called to explain the form and meaning of the liturgy and sacraments in a way that forms both the heart and mind of the learner.

3. **Catechesis promotes moral formation in Jesus Christ.** Catechists are called to teach others that to "clothe [ourselves] with . . . Christ" (Rom. 13:14, NIV) is to know and live the moral teachings of Christ. They are called to model and encourage faithful adherence to the demands of the gospel.

4. **Catechesis teaches the Christian how to pray with Christ.** Prayer and reflection are essential to the Christian interior life. Catechists are called to teach others to pray as Jesus prayed, helping them to understand that we encounter him in a special way through prayer and reflection.

5. **Catechesis prepares the Christian to live in community and to participate actively in the life and mission of the church.** Christ's teachings inform our interactions with others. Catechists are called to teach others that life in Christ is expressed through love for one another, humility, simplicity, and our concern and care for those in need. We are given the grace we need to fully participate in Jesus' mission.

6. **Catechesis promotes a missionary spirit that prepares the faithful to be present as Christians in society.** We live out our vocation in the world and can give witness to Jesus in many ways. Catechists are called to teach that at home, at school, at

social gatherings, or wherever we are, others should know we are Christians through our words and actions.

Help Me!

Notice how the first four tasks align with the four pillars of the *Catechism of the Catholic Church*. In his book *A Well-Built Faith*, page xiii, Joe Paprocki creatively introduces the pillars with the acronym HELP:

- **H**old on to our faith—Creed
- **E**xpress our faith—Liturgy and sacraments
- **L**ive our faith—Life in Christ (morality)
- **P**ray our faith—Prayer

The final two tasks are given the acronym ME:

- **M**entor our faith—Apprenticeship in Christian living
- **E**vangelize our faith—Promote a missionary spirit

As catechists look to us—their catechetical leader—and plead, "Help me!" we can be confident in knowing that the training and formation we offer will indeed help them to teach others because their teaching comes from Christ. As Jesus said, "My teaching is not my own. It comes from the one who sent me" (John 7:16, NIV).

Forming a Well-Rounded Catechist

- Catechist formation seeks to develop a well-rounded catechist. By that we mean a catechist who is capable of providing students with a holistic learning experience that balances cognition (knowing), affection (being), and behavior/performance (doing). We'll look more closely at these areas in chapter 6. In the meantime, however, it is important to know that before catechists even begin their ministry, they should receive initial formation that will assist them in grasping the very nature of catechesis, basic methodologies, and a basic understanding of the Six Tasks of Catechesis described earlier in this chapter.

- As they continue to participate in their ministry, encourage them to continue to grow in their knowledge of the Catholic faith, in their understanding of various methodologies, and in their mastery of the Six Tasks of Catechesis, shown above. Ongoing growth should focus on their formation on the human, spiritual, intellectual, and apostolic levels.

Provide Options

In today's fast-paced world, it is imperative that we offer catechist formation in a variety of ways that will help busy catechists get the training they need. Consider making use of the following options:

- local opportunities at your own or a neighboring parish (including resources that catechists can use independently at home, such as Webinars, podcasts, DVDs, and YouTube videos)
- regional opportunities (including offerings by a cluster of parishes, deanery, and vicariate)
- diocesan opportunities (including conferences, workshops, seminars, institutes, and retreats)
- online opportunities, such as the University of Dayton Virtual Learning Community for Faith Formation (VLCFF https://vlcff.udayton.edu/).

Another way to shape a well-rounded program is by scheduling it in. Some catechetical leaders take a unique approach to scheduling catechist formation so that it is seen as integral to their faith-formation program and not as something optional.

One parish, which holds faith-formation sessions weekly on Monday evenings, designates the first Monday of each month for catechist formation. The young people do not have classes on that evening, but catechists are required to attend. Since the formation sessions occur on the same evening that the catechists have set aside for teaching classes, attendance is excellent. Another parish does not begin children's faith-formation sessions until October, so that the entire month of September can be used for weekly catechist-formation experiences.

Connect Theory and Practice (praxis)

While a certificate program provides a great foundation, catechists—particularly those who are new—will need your guidance to form a *praxis*—putting into practice what they have learned, or, as the Jesuits are fond of saying, "a way of proceeding." Theology that is not rooted in sound and effective praxis will remain sterile. So while it may be tempting to hand your catechists their teaching textbooks, wish them good luck, and send them off to the classrooms, it is important to spend quality time mentoring them, acclimating them to the process, and strengthening their skills. After all, even with great teaching resources it takes time to internalize the lesson and develop a teaching *savoir faire*—an effective way of proceeding.

You can set up your catechists for success by considering the following ideas:

- My pastor and/or I regularly converse with catechists about their lessons, offering encouragement and direction.
- I provide or have access to the primary teaching resources they need, such as a Catholic Bible, the *Catechism of the Catholic Church*, the *General Directory for Catechesis*, and the *National Directory for Catechesis*.
- I offer adequate teaching aids, such as student textbooks, catechist guides, and classroom supplies.
- I give them current teaching resources, such as periodicals/magazines.

- I am in regular contact with the diocesan catechetical office and keep my catechists informed of available catechetical resources, retreats, and conferences.

Finally, guide your catechists through a simple lesson-planning process. These lesson plans need to have clearly stated learning outcomes that connect the catechist's guide to the diocesan standards, the liturgical year, and other parish/diocesan requirements. We'll touch upon this more in chapter 6.

For Reflection and Discussion: How do you support your catechists in their ministry, particularly those who are new?

Encourage Collaboration

Does all this sound overwhelming? It may be helpful to form planning groups in grade clusters (i.e., K–2; 3–5; 6–8; 9–12). Meet and collaborate with these groups regularly to pray together and review their lessons. Through this process, you will come to understand what is being planned, how catechists in each grade level are able to support one another, and in what areas they need ongoing formation.

An important advantage of these discussion groups is the discovery of emerging leaders. They will be the ones who are enthusiastic and consistently come prepared. They will ask questions beyond the operational aspects of lesson planning and present creative new ways to engage students and their parents. Nurture these catechists carefully—God has called them to ministry in a very special way: leadership!

Summary: "How Can I Understand Unless Someone Guides Me?"

Philip ran up [to the chariot] and heard him reading the prophet Isaiah. He asked, "Do you understand what you are reading?" He replied, "How can I, unless someone guides me?" And he invited Philip to get in and sit with him. (Acts 8:30–31)

Philip was sent by the Holy Spirit to lead others toward an ever-deepening understanding of the faith. The catechetical leader develops catechists in the same way. Today we hear a lot about people demanding their rights! If there were a "catechist's bill of rights," one of those rights would be training and formation. We owe it to our catechists to provide the very best training we can. It is their right, and we do them a disservice by ignoring their need for ongoing formation.

As a catechetical leader, do everything within your power to create a culture of ongoing learning and formation for catechists. Every time you gather with catechists, provide resources or information about opportunities for their own faith formation, and assist and support them in taking advantage of these opportunities. As far as your budget allows, provide financial assistance for catechists to attend workshops and seminars so they can benefit from all the training they deserve.

Growing as a Catechetical Leader

Before asking others to engage in formation, it helps to reflect on your own attitudes and behaviors. How well do you relate to these statements?

The Effective Catechetical Leader

Top-Ten List for a Catechist's Way of Proceeding

- Others seem to consider me to be an evangelizing catechetical minister—one who is joyful, inviting, and present to others on their journey of faith.

- I set an example for lifelong learning by regularly participating in classes and workshops offered through my local diocese, nationally, or online.

- I consider myself an avid reader of good Catholic literature and other resources.

- I continually challenge myself to uphold the true teachings of the Church, seeking creative and inviting ways to help students and their families connect faith and life.

- I understand that the catechetical program is an integral part of parish life.

Your good example makes a great impression on your catechists. You'll also be better equipped to encourage your catechists to complete their formation requirements and to mentor them toward best practices. Go to www.loyolapress.com/ECL to access the worksheet.

Suggested Action

Check with your own diocese to learn more about resources, requirements, and processes for catechist formation leading to certification.

Start at the local level by integrating catechist formation into every catechist meeting or gathering that you host. Encourage catechists to share creative ideas, resources, and approaches.

For Further Consideration

Beyond the Catechist's Toolbox. Joe Paprocki (Chicago: Loyola Press, 2013).

The Catechism of the Catholic Church and the Craft of Catechesis. Pierre de Cointet, Barbara Morgan, Petroc Willey, PhD (San Francisco: Ignatius Press, 2008).

31 Days to Becoming a Better Religious Educator. Jared Dees and Joe Paprocki (Notre Dame, IN: Ave Maria Press, 2013).

The Way God Teaches. Joseph D. White, PhD (Huntington, IN: Our Sunday Visitor, 2014).

5

Cultural Diversity: Mining the Rich Cultures of Catechists

The rich multicultural realities that we experience within our parishes across the United States is a blessing to the Catholic Church. It presents us with many opportunities to explore what it means to embrace God's gift of diversity and to strengthen and enliven the community of faith through celebrating the rich cultural heritages of our catechists.

In his book *Being Catholic: How We Believe, Practice and Think*, Archbishop Daniel E. Pilarczyk writes:

> It has been said that Catholicism is as much a culture as a religion. In this sense "culture" means an integrated pattern of knowledge, belief, and behavior that depends on experience and knowledge transmitted from one generation to another. It expresses the customary beliefs and social forms of a religious or social group. We all belong to one or more cultures: national, economic, ethnic; cultures determined by age and cultures determined by geography. The Catholic culture is a pattern of belief and behavior that gives us our identity as Catholic women and men, and "practicing" our Catholic faith means expressing who and what we are as members of the "Catholic culture," and, even more importantly, as members of the Catholic Church. (Cincinnati: St. Anthony Messenger Press, 2006, 89)

Ethnic Diversity

The United States is a country of immigrants. Accounts of American history testify to the millions of people around the world who have left their homelands for a chance to start new lives in this country—and they continue to come here today. For Catholics, the rich landscape of the church in the United States continues to change, with immigrants making up a considerable share of our population.

In its 2014 *Religious Landscape Study*, the Pew Research Center reported that Catholics are more likely than other Americans to be immigrants or children of immigrants. Here are their findings.

- More than a quarter of U.S. Catholic adults (27%) were born outside the country, compared with 15% of U.S. adults overall.
- Most of these Catholic immigrants (22% of all U.S. Catholics) are from elsewhere in the Americas.
- As of 2014, an additional 15% of Catholic Americans have at least one foreign-born parent.
- That leaves 57% of Catholics who were born in the U.S. to two native-born parents. By comparison, nearly three-quarters (74%) of American adults overall were born in the country to two U.S.-born parents.

The ethnic diversity of the church in the United States is indeed a blessing. It also presents us with the real challenge of fostering an openness to authentic, multicultural expressions of the Catholic faith. This process is referred to as "inculturation," and it begins with the people we invite to serve as catechists.

Inculturation: A Primer

So what exactly does inculturation mean? The Church uses the term *inculturation* to describe the missionary process of "listening to the culture of the people for an echo of the word of God" (*NDC*, #21C). This will entail discerning the presence of authentic gospel values in the culture as well as extending an invitation to come to faith. It is "a process that brings the transforming power of the Gospel to touch persons in their hearts and cultures at their deepest levels" (*NDC*, #25F).

God's saving grace is present and at work in all cultures. So rather than attempt to form a "common culture," we instead recognize that a common ground exists in all cultures for the truth of the gospel. As one may imagine, this process takes time and is highly relational. It requires us to be a welcoming presence, one who speaks *with* others and not just at them.

The Parish Experience

Culture (the root word in *inculturation*) is commonly defined as a group of people who share common values and beliefs. These common values may be influenced by our ethnic heritage, the generation into which we are born, the region in which we are raised, and much more. We need to offer catechists some formation experiences to which they can relate and through which their unique contributions are valued.

How can we create a welcoming environment for these catechists, one that encourages an authentic expression of their faith in light of the gospel and leads to their fuller participation and growth? Jesus modeled this action in his own ministry by developing relationships, listening to stories, and unveiling God's salvation at work in the lives of those he encountered. Meaningful storytelling not only is informative but also enables us to discover each other's unique gifts and promote a global family atmosphere of brothers and sisters in Christ.

A Place to Call Home

Antonio lifted a single suitcase from the baggage carousel at the airport's international terminal and set it gently at his feet. He offered a prayer of thanksgiving, grateful that the lengthy journey from his tropical village was finally complete. A beloved and well-respected educator in his home country, Antonio had accepted a teaching position for a school in the United States and was determined to work hard to help his students succeed and provide much-needed financial support for his siblings and aging parents back home.

His relatives greeted him warmly, excited to introduce him to American life. Antonio fondly recalled: "From the airport, we drove straight to a nearby restaurant. Large bowls of soup were placed in front of each person at the table. I couldn't believe the bounty! Back home, one bowl of soup would have to feed my entire family."

"I couldn't help it . . . tears flowed from my eyes. I felt grateful for the generous amount of food yet downhearted thinking about how hard my family had to work in order to provide the kind of feast that I was about to enjoy. When we reached my relatives' home, I was shown to their guest room. Imagine that—an extra room with an extra bed to welcome the weary traveler. Not even our Blessed Mother and Saint Joseph received such a welcome on the eve of their Son's birth. Again, I was astounded."

"The inspiration came to me that night after praying the Holy Rosary: I committed to becoming actively involved in the corporal works of mercy in my new homeland. I wanted to make sure that other people do not feel alienated, have a place to call home and food to eat."

For Reflection and Discussion: What gifts does Antonio bring to the church in the United States? What gifts would he bring to a parish as a catechist?

Tina's Story

Growing up I was raised primarily as a Southern Baptist. As an African American living in the South, I had limited exposure to the Catholic faith because, frankly, there weren't many Catholics where I lived. I met my husband, a Catholic, when we both were college students. After dating for a while we began to discuss marriage and having a family together. I agreed that our future children would be raised in the Catholic faith because I understood how important this was to him. For a while I remained Baptist, attending Mass with my husband in addition to services at the Baptist church.

In our Baptist church we praise and give God glory through song. And we're very enthusiastic about it! When I first began attending the Catholic Mass, everything seemed so silent and somber. There was no clapping and no gospel choir. I recall looking over at my husband and thinking that he looked like a lump on a log while praying. But what touched my heart as I learned more about the Catholic faith was the Eucharist. It was not a "reminder" or a "representation" of Jesus. It *is* the Body and Blood of Jesus. That is what struck me as different—it made sense to me that Christ could be truly present in the Eucharist. And eventually I began to understand that God was calling me to start the process of becoming Catholic.

My experience of the catechumenate was very interesting. I began with a group of twenty-four persons and in the end, I was the only one who completed the process. I suppose it could have been a disappointing experience for me to be the last person standing, but I had an amazing pastor and RCIA coordinator who supported me, and naturally, I received a lot of personal attention!

By now, my husband was an active-duty officer in the military. Anywhere in the world his tours of duty took us I was comforted by the consistency, the universal practice, of the Catholic Mass, the readings in the three liturgical cycles, the Lenten and Easter seasons, and so on. No matter the country, the language, or the culture, I knew I could follow along and be "fed" by Christ in his word and in the Eucharist.

But it wasn't until a tour of duty brought us back to the South that I felt I had come full circle. My family and I attended Mass at a Catholic parish that served primarily African-American families. The liturgies incorporated a gospel-choir musical style that was incredibly good. I felt validated—I could sing God's praises in a style that touched my heart *and* I was able to receive the Eucharist. For me, it was a perfect balance.

My husband and I have raised our beautiful family and are now retired from the military and settled into a place that we will call home for years to come. I love our new parish. Our priests are great. We are warmly welcomed by our fellow parishioners. People are genuinely happy to see us. They ask about our children. They personally invite us to participate in celebrations and other parish events. We are a diverse yet tight-knit community, and there is even an energetic choir who inspires us to lift our voices in praise of God.

Yet even in this diverse setting my husband and I are the only African-American parishioners there (we're working on this!), and I find that it still can be easy for people to stereotype and assume things about us. So it's important to have a sense of humor and be very patient as we come to know and understand each other. As an example, I tell folks not to assume that I can sing or that I will be in the choir. God gave me talents, but singing is not one of them!

The beauty of this is that as they come to know us better, we come to know them better as well. We break down stereotypes and assumptions on both sides as we discover common ground. My Catholic faith has deepened through this community, and we really consider ourselves blessed.

For Reflection and Discussion: What gifts does Tina bring to the church? What gifts would she bring to a parish as a catechist?

Catherine, A Young-Adult Perspective

I'd say the motto of our young-adult culture is "Do what you love, and love what you do." It's the message that we grew up with, and it came with over-the-top expectations. Most of these expectations started in childhood: be a high achiever in primary and high school, get into a good college (with scholarships), strive to obtain a lucrative job that aligns with your college major, etc. We are expected to take big risks to fulfill big dreams. For many of us it means holding down a string of jobs, always willing at a moment's notice to go on to the next best thing because we believe we are masters of our own destiny. I guess you could say that we are driven by a thirst to "do what we love and love what we do." But it seems we're always thirsty.

Of course, we are not masters of our own destiny, and no amount of worldly success can quench our thirst, because what we really thirst for is God. God gives me living water when I go to Mass, pray, and help others. God quenches my thirst when I accept that I am not the master of my own destiny and can't do it all myself. My new motto is inspired by our Blessed Mother: Love God and "do whatever he tells you" (John 2:5).

For Reflection and Discussion: What gifts does Catherine, who identifies with the young-adult culture, bring to the church in the United States? What gifts would she bring to a parish as a catechist?

Each of these stories provides us insights into the words of Saint Pope John Paul II: "The Church makes the gospel incarnate in different cultures and at the same time introduces peoples, together with their cultures, into her own community; she transmits to them her own values, at the same time taking the good elements that already exist in them and renewing them from within" (*Guide for Catechists*, Vatican, 1993).

Building Intercultural Competence

How may we go about learning the process of inculturation in a systematic way? The USCCB offers five learning principles to guide us.

1. Frame issues of diversity in terms of the Church's identity and mission to evangelize. Inculturation is not political correctness; it is an expression of the Body of Christ.

2. Seek an understanding of culture and how it works. Cultures have ideas, behaviors, beliefs, values, languages, rules, traditions, and ways of celebrating, eating, and dressing. Intercultural

competence begins by communicating, relating, and working across cultural boundaries.

3. Develop intercultural communication skills in pastoral settings. We need to learn skills to more effectively minister in situations with groups of differing cultures, taking into consideration such things as body language, silence, proximity, contact, expressions of emotion, and so on.

4. Expand one's knowledge of the obstacles that impede effective intercultural relations. We need to be honest about the reality of racism, racial insensitivity, prejudice, and stereotypes and the underlying fears, ignorance, and guilt that accompany these.

5. Foster ecclesial integration rather than assimilation in Church settings, with a spirituality of reconciliation and mission. Our diversity as a Church is not a problem to be overcome but is a gift to be celebrated and an expression of our communion. http://www.usccb.org/issues-and-action/cultural-diversity/ intercultural-competencies/ intercultural-competencies-training-of-trainers-program.cfm.

If you as a catechetical leader will pay attention to these principles of inculturation, especially when recruiting catechists, it will help you and your parish to

- tap into the vitality of emerging new groups,
- incorporate the gifts of other cultures and advance the process of giving and receiving among all God's people, and
- establish a foundation for mutual acceptance and trust among diverse communities present in the parish.

(*Building Intercultural Competence for Ministers*, USCCB)

The USCCB offers modules on Building Intercultural Competencies for Ministers on its Web site, www.usccb.org.

Practical Applications

In book 6 of this series, we will further explore inculturation in terms of focusing on those to be catechized. For the purposes of this book, with our focus on the vocation of the catechist, it's important to begin our efforts of inculturation by assembling a team of catechists that truly reflects the diversity of those we serve.

At your catechist gatherings, invite catechists to share their stories, expressing how they have come to know God through their own cultures. Stories provide a familiar starting point for evangelization and catechesis. Here are some prompts you can use to jump-start such storytelling.

- Reflect upon your story of faith. Who influenced you and why?
- What are some prayers/traditions/rituals of the Catholic faith in your culture that you treasure? Why are they important to you?
- What cultural celebrations or artistic expressions (music, dance, art) inspire you on your journey of faith?

Diverse cultural expressions are a gift to the parish community. Receive these gifts, but be sure that plans to integrate elements of a culture are made in collaboration with the "cultural natives." Do not presume you understand the proper use of a prayer, song, or ritual. If you have doubts, simply ask those of a specific ethnic or cultural background to share their understanding of their own tradition.

Summary: "How Is It That We Each Hear Them in Our Own Language?"

All of them were filled with the Holy Spirit and began to speak in other languages, as the Spirit gave them ability. Now there were devout Jews from every nation under heaven living in Jerusalem. And at this sound, the crowd gathered and was bewildered, because each one heard them speaking in the native language of each. Amazed and astonished, they asked, "Are not all these who are speaking Galileans? And how is it that we hear, each of us, in our own native language?" (Acts 2:4–8)

In Acts 2, we see how the Holy Spirit made it possible for the disciples to preach the gospel to people from every nation. God embraced the different cultures. What a remarkable miracle! Just as on the day of Pentecost, so today the Spirit will enable you to reach across cultures and engage others.

Catechesis is a multifaceted evangelizing activity of the church that is made stronger by an emphasis on the wonderful diversity of the Body of Christ. Fostering vocations to the ministry of catechesis requires an awareness of the ethnic and cultural diversity of our community. As a catechetical leader, you are called to celebrate the cultural diversity of your catechists, promote inculturation of the gospel message, and foster vocations to the ministry of catechesis by drawing from the unique ethnic and cultural gifts of your parish community.

Growing as a Catechetical Leader

Our Church is *catholic*, meaning that it is universal—gathering all peoples without exception. As such, we are called to unity, not uniformity. Take some time to reflect on how you have experienced and been enriched by the diversity of the Church. How are you reaching out to all peoples without exception? What does it mean for you to strive for unity but not uniformity?

Go to www.loyolapress.com/ECL to access the worksheet.

Suggested Action

For most Christians, the way we pray and worship is very personal and is heavily influenced by our culture. In particular, the music we use to worship is often closely connected to our ethnicity. Begin compiling a playlist of hymns from various ethnic and cultural backgrounds to use whenever you gather catechists for prayer and worship.

For Further Consideration

Best Practices for Shared Parishes: So That All May Be One (USCCB, 2014).

Building Intercultural Competence for Ministers (USCCB, 2012).

Leading a Healthy Multi-Ethnic Church: Seven Common Challenges and How to Overcome Them. Mark DeYmaz and Harry Li (Grand Rapids, MI: Zondervan, 2012).

One Church, Many Cultures: The Good News of Cultural Diversity (USCCB, e-newsletter, fall/winter 2016).

6

Care and Feeding: Ongoing Formation of Catechists

As we have said before, the Church owes it to catechists to provide high-quality formation that will help them develop into well-rounded catechists. Such formation is designed to help them grow in their own relationship with the Lord, in knowledge of the Catholic faith, and in methodologies and techniques for effectively engaging participants in catechetical experiences that lead not only to the transmission of information but also to an encounter with Christ that leads to transformation.

Offering the Essentials

That said, the truth is that it can be very challenging to convince catechists of the importance of ongoing faith formation! Aside from being very busy people who often find it difficult to find time to attend or participate in ongoing formation, catechists also have their own preconceived notions about the value of ongoing formation. Here are three examples:

Catechist 1: I don't feel that I need to attend any of the ongoing formation classes on teaching methodology. I have a degree in religious studies and know more than any of the other catechists. I'm sure I won't learn anything new, and I think it will just be a waste of time. My students can recite their prayers and have memorized many passages from the Bible and the Catechism, which will serve them for life. There is so much information they need to know that we don't have time for hands-on activities.

Catechist 2: I've been attending ongoing formation classes but feel that they are so rigid. I think that all I need to do is to teach the students how to pray, read Scripture together, and share stories of faith. I'm sure they have a hard time relating to the *Catechism of the Catholic Church* and other formal doctrines of the Church. I just want them to feel good about being Catholic and come to know the joy of the gospel.

Catechist 3: I wonder if our ongoing formation classes could include ideas for outreach. I think students need less time learning about the Church and more time doing church. We need to go beyond the parish and out to the community to evangelize.

Have you picked up on the pattern? The catechists above express a tendency toward certain priorities: catechist 1—knowledge of the faith; catechist 2—how a person feels about the faith in his/her very being; catechist 3—what a person is to *do* given what he/she believes. Contemporary education models describe learning in three domains: cognitive, affective, and behavioral. Simply put, they describe a holistic approach to a quality education.

- Cognitive: mental skills/knowledge
- Affective: attitudes, motivations, values
- Behavioral: physical or manual skills

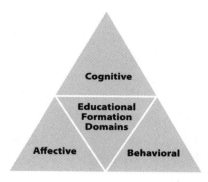

These domains apply to both adult and child educational programs. By listening to how catechists express their personal learning preferences, we are often able to gain insights into their teaching preferences and priorities. Catechist 1 focused on the cognitive domain; catechist 2, the affective; and catechist 3, the behavioral. Each held a narrow point of view of what was necessary for the catechetical experience of the learner.

The truth is, each of the three holds only one piece of the entire puzzle that makes for a holistic approach to faith formation. In the *General Directory for Catechesis* (#238), the bishops of the Church tell us that formation, especially for catechists, must be three-dimensional, covering the areas of "knowing, being, and *savoir-faire* (a style of doing)."

Being, Knowing, and Doing

Ongoing formation in faith certainly involves increasing one's knowledge of sacred Scripture and the Sacred Tradition of the Catholic Church. This knowledge, along with one's Christian self-awareness, beliefs, and values, influences one's actions. But there is so much more to it. The goal is not simply to become a better catechist but to become a better person: to *be* in Christ, to *know* Christ more intimately, and to *do* as Christ did—to be a saint!

When offering ongoing formation for your catechists, it is crucial that you offer them the whole puzzle with all three pieces. The following are some ways you can do that:

- **Being:** formation that helps catechists to discover their vocation and to mature as people, believers, and apostles. Formation in this area takes the shape of retreats, days, mornings, afternoons, or evenings of reflection, spiritual direction/companioning, prayer groups, and resources and opportunities to enrich the catechist's prayer life and spirituality. Topics to be addressed might include but are not limited to

  - personal prayer
  - prayer methods (Daily Examen, *lectio divina*, centering prayer, Liturgy of the Hours, etc.)
  - devotions (rosary, novenas, Chaplet of Divine Mercy, etc.)
  - spirituality
  - devotion to Mary and the saints
  - devotion to the Eucharist (liturgy, adoration of the Blessed Sacrament, etc.)

- **Knowing:** formation that helps catechists embrace their faith by acquiring sufficient knowledge of the faith they are called to proclaim. Formation in this area takes the shape of workshops, seminars, institutes, conferences, and resources designed to deepen the catechist's knowledge of the Catholic faith. Topics to be addressed might include but are not limited to

- The Trinity
- Christology
- Church (ecclesiology, history, Mary and the saints)
- Catholic social teaching
- Sacraments and liturgy
- Morality and conscience formation
- Prayer and worship
- Scripture
- Evangelization

- **Doing:** formation that helps catechists more effectively transmit the message of the gospel and creatively engage learners. Formation in this area takes the shape of workshops, seminars, institutes, conferences, and resources designed to broaden and sharpen the catechist's skills and techniques in various catechetical methodologies. Topics to be addressed might include but are not limited to

  - lesson planning
  - methodologies and learning activities
  - learning styles
  - preparing the learning environment
  - handling discipline
  - leading prayer
  - using catechetical resources and technology
  - doing assessment

The Eucharist Is at the Center

An essential aspect of ongoing formation is found in the richness of Catholic sacramental life. In the fifth century, Saint Augustine described a sacrament as "an outward and visible sign of an inward and invisible grace." It is through the sacraments that we can help remind catechists of the wondrous ways in which God's grace is at work in our lives and in the Church. These include

- Regular participation in the sacramental life of the Church, especially the Eucharist.
- Attention to personal prayer and liturgical celebrations.
- Online formation resources and opportunities, such as the "3-Minute Retreat" and "Sunday Connection" by Loyola Press or resources available from Creighton University's Online Ministries.

Providing catechists with opportunities to share their stories of sacramental life taps into familiar territory, particularly when focusing on the sacraments of initiation. Catechists are personally involved with preparing young people for baptism, confirmation, and Eucharist, and are continually deepening their own relationships with Christ through these sacraments. Their love for the sacraments can provide meaningful ongoing formation experiences.

The Eucharist stands as the source and summit of the spiritual life of the catechist, as with all Catholics. Catechists are called to have a deep devotion to the Eucharist—the sacrament that nourishes us and reminds us that it is Christ who empowers and compels us in our catechetical ministry despite our own unworthiness. For Catholics, Jesus Christ is encountered in many ways, but none more powerful than in the Eucharist. For catechists, this encounter with Christ in the Eucharist enables them to, in turn, invite those they teach to encounter the Lord in this intimate manner. As a catechetical leader, you can offer no greater assistance to your catechists than by fostering a devotion to the Eucharist and cultivating a hunger for Jesus in the Eucharist. This can be done, of course, by offering them opportunities to receive Christ in the Eucharist at Mass but also through the practice of adoration before the Blessed Sacrament—something that can be done before or after a catechist meeting or catechetical session.

For Reflection and Discussion: Of the three learning domains—cognitive, affective, behavioral—do your catechists exhibit a tendency toward one in particular? How might they achieve greater balance?

A Catechist's Story

My father is a gifted gardener who has a particular talent for growing fruit trees. First, he decides what, when, and where to plant. Then he prepares the soil, plants the seedlings, nurtures them carefully, and protects them from invasion. Later they bear delicious and healthful fruit.

As a teen, I recall watching him prune one of the fruit trees and asking, "Dad, do you talk to your trees?"

He replied, "Yes, I do."

"What do you say to them?"

He replied with a grin, "I tell them, 'If you don't bear good fruit, I'm going to chop you down!'"

That day, through my father's wit and wisdom, I suddenly made a connection between the gifts and fruits of the Holy Spirit. The seven gifts of the Holy Spirit are given to us in baptism and strengthened in confirmation. By using these gifts for God's purposes, our lives bear fruit.

This story highlights the catechist's connection to the gifts and fruits of the Holy Spirit. She tells of the ways in which they are part of her inner transformation as a Christian and continued inspiration for her

"Christlikeness." Indeed, all catechists need and deserve opportunities for ongoing faith formation to help them grow in Christ.

Program Considerations

Planning high-quality faith-formation experiences with flexible options requires a bit of forethought.

Start by forming a team to assess the needs of your catechists and by developing short- and long-term program goals. The parish, parish school, vicariate, and/or diocese offer many opportunities for ongoing formation, from Advent/Lenten missions to faith-formation conferences. Encourage your catechists to attend these learning experiences, and accompany them as often as possible.

While it is desirable for faith formation to take place in-person, it is not always practical. If one or two catechists find it difficult to meet in person, consider including them through the use of technology, from live Webinars launched from a mobile device to recorded audio and/or video presentations.

Finally, communicate with your catechists, giving them ample time to plan ahead. Be consistent with your gathering dates/times, and regularly publish an updated, ongoing formation calendar.

Summary: "Apart from Me You Can Do Nothing"

"I am the vine; you are the branches. If you remain in me and I in you, you will bear much fruit; apart from me you can do nothing." (John 15:5, NIV)

Catechists must stay connected to the Vine! It is common among those in catechetical ministry to hear the phrase, "You can't give what you don't have." For catechists, what we are called to give is a relationship with Jesus Christ. In order for us to be able to give this gift to others, we must ourselves be in relationship with the Lord.

As a catechetical leader, one of your key responsibilities is to keep your catechists connected to the Vine through ongoing formation. Formation is not a task to be completed; it is a way of life that places encounter with Jesus at the forefront and center. As you seek to provide ongoing formation for your catechists, be sure to offer a variety of options and provide formation that pays attention to the three aspects of being, knowing, and doing.

Growing as a Catechetical Leader

As you look at the three dimensions of formation—being, knowing, and doing—with respect to your position as a catechetical leader, which area do you feel most or least equipped in? What will you do to move things to the next step?

Go to www.loyolapress.com/ECL to access the worksheet.

Suggested Action

As mentioned earlier, it is good practice to set up a formation calendar that extends twelve to eighteen months ahead. Create a chart with three categories across the top of the page: Being, Knowing, and Doing, and twelve to eighteen categories down the left side for the months you are planning to offer formation. Work with your catechists to create a plan that is reasonable and practical, yet thorough.

For Further Consideration

Being: *The Catechist's Backpack.* Joe Paprocki and Julianne Stanz (Chicago: Loyola Press, 2015); *The Spirituality of the Catechist.*

Janet Schaeffler, OP (New London, CT: Twenty-Third Publications, 2014).

Knowing: *Love Unveiled.* Edward Sri (San Francisco: Ignatius Press, 2015); *This Is Our Faith.* Michael Pennock (Notre Dame, IN: Ave Maria Press, 1998); *A Well-Built Faith.* Joe Paprocki and Doug Hall (Chicago: Loyola Press, 2008).

Doing: *Beyond the Catechist's Toolbox.* Joe Paprocki (Chicago: Loyola Press, 2013); *Catechist 101.* Carole M. Eipers (New London, CT: Twenty-Third Publications, 2014); *The Catechist's Toolbox.* Joe Paprocki and Doug Hall (Chicago: Loyola Press, 2007); *Here's How: A Catechist's Guide.* Lee Danesco (New London, CT: Twenty-Third Publications, 2014); *31 Days to Becoming a Better Religious Educator.* Jared Dees and Joe Paprocki (Notre Dame: Ave Maria Press, 2013).

7

Doing It "By the Book": Supervision, Evaluation, and Record Keeping

Serving in catechetical ministry is a spiritual calling. Yet there are also very practical aspects to ministry that leaders must learn about. We need to employ effective strategies for supervising, evaluating, and keeping records of each catechist. In this way, we can enhance the formation of our catechists and pass on helpful records to our successors for them to build on.

Building for Success

Scenario 1

It was a beautiful Sunday morning, and the weekly parish catechetical sessions were well under way. Sister Janet, the catechetical leader, began her customary walk through the classrooms. Earlier in the month she had conducted a workshop to help her catechists plan their lessons for the upcoming season of Lent. However, due to a scheduling conflict, catechist Mr. Leonard was unable to attend. Sister Janet shared the desired learning outcomes with him over the phone and discussed resources that he could use to help students meet the outcomes. Yet despite Sr. Janet's multiple requests, he had yet to turn in his lesson plans. Whenever she asked about them, he assured her that he'd get them to her soon.

On the first Sunday of Lent, Sr. Janet entered Mr. Leonard's fifth-grade classroom. She noted with delight that the students were quite engaged in an activity. Upon closer examination, she discovered that they all were painting designs on smooth little stones. Although she couldn't understand the purpose of the activity, she didn't want to correct Mr. Leonard in the middle of his class. She looked forward to learning how he had integrated this activity into helping prepare the children for the sacrament of reconciliation, which was the student learning objective for this particular lesson during the Lenten season.

After the children were dismissed, Sr. Janet approached Mr. Leonard. "I noticed that your students were quite engaged in an activity today. Why were they decorating stones?"

Mr. Leonard replied enthusiastically, "Because I thought it would be fun for them."

"What was the point of the lesson?" asked Sr. Janet.

"To have fun so they would enjoy coming to class every week."

"I'm glad they enjoyed the activity. How did it help to prepare the students for confession?"

"Hmm . . ."

Scenario 2

The day after the lesson-planning workshop, Sr. Janet received a call from catechist Mrs. Fujimoto.

"Sr. Janet, during our catechist meetings we had discussed the importance of parent involvement. The season of Lent starts soon, so I'm calling for your permission to invite several parents to assist me in the classroom during the Lenten season."

On the first Sunday of Lent, Sr. Janet entered Mrs. Fujimoto's third-grade classroom. The children were gathered in several small groups. In each group a volunteer parent was reading sacred Scripture from a children's Bible and leading children in discussion. Later in the lesson, the children were gathered into one large group and were taught a Lenten song and sacred gestures.

After the children were dismissed, Sr. Janet approached Mrs. Fujimoto. "I noticed that your students were quite engaged in their lesson today and that several parents were also involved. What was the point of the lesson?"

"During our lesson-planning workshop, we discussed the main learning outcomes for students during Lent. Today's lesson focused on helping the students know and love God even more by preparing them for the Gospel reading that they will hear during Mass. And by having parents directly involved in reading and discussion groups, they learn how to discuss and even sing the gospel message with their own children. It's a win-win!"

Supervision Is Not Micromanagement

When we hear the term *supervision*, it's easy to conjure up visions of a kindergarten playground monitor whose responsibility is to watch over the children like a hawk. The thing is, our catechists are not little children. They are our brothers and sisters in Christ and collaborators in our shared ministry! Thus, the purpose of supervision is not to micromanage but to listen to, communicate with, and motivate catechists toward success. In your role as a catechetical leader, supervision is one of the most effective ways you can ensure that sound catechesis is taking place, while also contributing to the ongoing growth and development of your catechists.

While everyone has his or her own unique style, consider the following basic rules or principles for supervising catechists:

- **Volunteers are "unpaid" staff.** Whether receiving a wage or not, every catechetical minister has a role and responsibility that contribute to the mission of the Church, and thus, it is proper for that work to be supervised to ensure quality.

- **Catechists are essential to the success of your faith-formation program.** They are a precious human resource for whom we must be grateful. To the extent that the parish is able, invest in them by giving of your time and by providing adequate resources to help them be successful.
- **Supervision is about relationship building.** There's a saying in the corporate world: people leave managers, not corporations. In the same way, catechists often leave catechetical leaders, not programs. While you can't please everyone, focusing on building and nurturing relationships with catechists is of major importance. The last thing you want to do is to assign them their duties and leave them alone.
- **Love them.** Be a model of God's love and compassion. Take a personal interest in them. Always seek to find common ground.
- **Include both informal and formal supervision.** Informal supervision consists of the brief and unscheduled "drop in" visit, while formal supervision is scheduled and includes observation of an entire lesson.
- The late, great baseball Hall of Famer Yogi Berra once said, "You can observe a lot by watching," and you can do a lot of watching and observing by walking around. Many managers and supervisors practice the art of "coaching by walking around," which gives them a firsthand opportunity to see how things are going.

When doing supervision of your catechists, it is important to have a clear sense of instructional and program goals, to establish a clear and consistent evaluation process, and to follow through with training and support.

For Reflection and Discussion: How would you describe your style and frequency of catechist supervision? What are your strengths and areas for improvement?

Instructional and Program Goals

Whatever their level of teaching expertise, catechists appreciate guidance in formulating instructional goals and lesson plans. Supervise the process with your catechists to ensure they follow required catechetical guidelines. Working together helps maintain content alignment throughout your entire program, and it reinforces a sense of purpose, collaboration, and belonging.

Supervision also involves establishing program goals and providing action steps for achieving them. Following are some examples:

Goal: Catechists are to have a basic understanding of Catholic teaching, Scripture, and Catholic tradition.
Action steps:

- Complete the diocesan catechist-certification program within the prescribed time frame.
- Participate in the annual retreat for catechists.
- Attend Mass regularly.

Goal: Catechists are to have honest and caring relationships with young people and their parents.
Action steps:

- Treat learners with respect at all times.
- Exercise patience and compassion.
- Communicate regularly with parents.

Goals:

- Catechists are to address the Six Tasks of Catechesis (NDC #20) within each catechetical year.
- Catechists are to exhibit effective teaching techniques and strategies.

- Catechists are to follow the policies and procedures outlined in the catechist handbook.

Action steps:

- Attend lesson-planning and teaching-method sessions offered by the parish and/or diocese.
- Submit lesson plans each month.
- Know the Six Tasks of Catechesis and address each during the catechetical year.
- Focus lessons on student learning outcomes (performance).
- Use teaching methods and assessments that are creative and age appropriate.
- Arrive for class prepared and on time.

Clearly articulated and agreed-upon goals as well as action steps set a positive tone for supervision because expectations are clear for both the catechist and the catechetical leader. To assist the catechists in meeting their goals, consider doing the following:

- Create a master calendar for the entire catechetical year. Note all regular instructional days, special-instructional days (for special liturgies, program- or parish-wide activities, etc.), and holidays.
- Provide access to workshops on lesson planning, classroom management, and communication skills.
- Provide recommendations on ways to enliven lessons by connecting learning objectives to parish life and the greater community.

Recall that the role of catechists is to enter into the journey of faith with their learners and their families in order to walk with them, teach them, and help them to recognize that Jesus is vibrantly alive, living among and within us. Thus, the ultimate purpose of supervision is to ensure that a Christ-centered learning environment is being provided and that quality, Christ-centered catechesis is taking place.

The Evaluation Process

It's important to make a distinction between an evaluation form and an evaluation process. We're all familiar with evaluation forms that are designed to provide information—in fact, a sample is provided later in this chapter. In contrast, the evaluation process is designed to be transformational. Think about the evaluation process in terms of a journey of four steps: assess, give feedback, evaluate, follow through.

Step 1: Assess

Assessment is an information-gathering process to develop an understanding of how well goals are being met. We gather this information from multiple sources, such as listening to participant and parent feedback, conducting regular visits to the classroom, and speaking directly with the catechist.

Step 2: Give Feedback

What is feedback? It is basically information about how we are doing in achieving a goal or an outcome. Sometimes feedback is an internal process, when I, not another person, decide whether a particular goal was achieved. For example, I train for a ten-kilometer race with the goal of feeling healthier in the process. Or I tell a humorous story with the goal of making people laugh, and I observe their reaction—whether they laugh out loud or politely chuckle.

Feedback on whether a goal has been achieved can also be external and more direct.

- A friend tells me, "When you took the time to plan a birthday celebration for me, I was really touched."

- My pastor says to me, "After the presentation you gave on the sacrament of reconciliation, I noticed that more families showed up for confession this month."
- My catechetical leader tells me, "Since you attended the lesson-planning workshop, you have regularly submitted your weekly lesson plans."

Note that in all cases, feedback consisted of a goal/desired outcome and an action that produced an effect. Giving feedback is not the same as giving advice or instructions, nor is it a judgment or an evaluation.

Let's examine how Sr. Janet might provide feedback to catechists Mr. Leonard and Mrs. Fujimoto.

"Mr. Leonard, to prepare the students for the sacrament of reconciliation during Lent (*goal/outcome*), you had them paint stones (action). But they tell me they didn't have time to learn the Act of Contrition or do an examination of conscience before going to confession (*effect*)."

"Mrs. Fujimoto, to prepare the students for liturgy during Lent (*goal/outcome*), you chose to have parents lead children in Scripture reflection and discussion, as well as familiarize them with the liturgical hymns through sacred gesture (*action*). The students said that all the activities helped them and their parents feel closer to Jesus (*effect*)."

These feedback statements do not judge the catechist's performance, nor do they provide advice or instructions. They simply provide a clear statement of what was the intended goal/outcome, the action in response to the goal, and the effect of that action. Thus, feedback provides the basis for later evaluating the catechist and his or her performance.

Step 3: Evaluate

Although it is the responsibility of the catechetical leader to conduct an evaluation, it is good practice for the catechist to play an active role in the process. This can be accomplished by having the catechist complete a self-evaluation and referring to it often during the formal evaluation. Use goals and action steps to create a catechist self-evaluation process. For example,

Goal: Catechists are to have a basic understanding of Catholic teaching, Scripture, and Catholic tradition.
Catechist input:

- Diocesan catechist-certification-program progress
- Attendance at annual catechist retreat
- Regular Mass attendance

Goal: Catechists are to have honest and caring relationships with young people and their parents.
Catechist input:

- I treat students with respect at all times.
- I exercise patience and compassion when students misbehave.
- I communicate regularly and have a positive relationship with parents.

Goals:

- Catechists are to address the Six Tasks of Catechesis within each school year.
- Catechists are to exhibit effective teaching techniques and strategies.
- Catechists are to follow the policies and procedures outlined in the handbook.

Catechist input:

- I attend lesson-planning and teaching-method sessions offered by the parish and/or diocese.
- I submit lesson plans each month.
- I focus lessons on student learning objectives (performance).
- I address the Six Tasks of Catechesis during the catechetical year.
- I use teaching methods and assessments that are creative and age appropriate.
- I arrive for class prepared and on time.

Because we love and appreciate our catechists, we want them to feel appreciated and affirmed. A formal evaluation is pleasant when catechists are making steady progress toward or are achieving their goals. Having an honest and direct conversation about areas of needed improvement, however, can be challenging. Here are some dos and don'ts for holding a formal evaluation.

- Do provide your pastor with a summary of the evaluations, including what goals are being met, key areas for improvement, how you plan to assist the catechists in their ongoing formation and growth, and additional resources, if necessary, that are needed in order to achieve desired end results.
- Do maintain copies of all catechist evaluations in your catechetical records.
- Do begin your evaluation session with prayer. This reminds both parties that Christ is present whenever two or three are gathered in his name. It also sets a proper pastoral tone.
- Do strive for clarity if you don't understand what the catechist is saying about his/her progress/performance: "Let me rephrase what I believe I heard you say." (Then in your own words, say what you heard.) "I'm not sure I follow you. Will you give me a

specific example of how you accomplished that goal or completed that action step?"

- Do strive for common ground if you do not agree with the catechist's self-evaluation: "Tell me more about how you arrived at that conclusion." "Thanks for sharing your point of view. Now let me share my perspective on that issue."

- Don't apologize for pointing out areas for improvement. "As catechists, we always strive to improve our skills. Based upon our conversation, here are one or two areas I'd like you to focus on." "I appreciate the honesty of your self-evaluation. Let's discuss one or two areas for improvement that you would like to focus on."

- Don't feel you need to answer all questions or address all issues during the session. "Your question about selecting a new textbook for next school year is a good one. Let's bring up the issue at our next catechist meeting and solicit input from the others." "Your plans for parent catechetical sessions sound interesting. Please put your plans in writing, and we'll discuss it further."

- Don't forget to follow through.

Step 4: Follow Through

Through the evaluation process you will discover the catechist's areas of strength and areas for growth and improvement. The evaluation is not the final word. It would be a mistake to believe that the conversation that took place during the formal evaluation is enough to spark improvement. Just because a catechist has gained insight into the behaviors that need to be addressed does not mean he/she has the ability or motivation to change.

Remember to collaborate with the catechist to create an action plan for improvement. Including resources and time lines is helpful

in ensuring that the catechist receives needed support and is held accountable.

For Reflection and Discussion: Catechist evaluation was described as a four-step process—assess, give feedback, evaluate, follow through. Describe the step(s) that you execute well and those that are an opportunity for growth.

Record Keeping

As a catechetical leader, you are basically the chief "archivist" of the faith-formation experiences of the parish. In many cases, you are required to maintain specific catechetical records, and we will explore this in more detail in book 5 of this series. In the meantime, however, it is important for you to know about the record keeping you are asked to do with regards to your catechists.

Safe Environment

The *Charter for the Protection of Children and Young People* was established by the USCCB in June 2002 to address allegations of sexual abuse of minors by Catholic clergy. The Charter includes guidelines for the prevention of future acts of abuse by clergy and all church workers. For many parishes, the ministry leaders, including the catechetical leaders, are responsible for identifying adults who require safe-environment background screening and training and for keeping records of their completion. The catechetical leader is also largely responsible for following the diocesan safe-environment education policy for children and youth.

Individual Catechist Files

It is important to keep an individual file on each of your catechists. This is especially helpful when transitions take place from one parish catechetical leader to another. Consider including the following information in each catechist's file:

- Personal information: legal name, address, emergency contact information
- Academic credentials, if applicable
- Special awards/recognitions
- Catechist formation/certification record
- Safe-environment certification
- Sample lesson plans
- Catechist meeting/workshop/retreat attendance
- Evaluations
- Communication logs

Consult your diocesan catechetical office for guidelines on the length of time information is to be kept on file, but records are typically kept for five years before being shredded. Catechist information should be considered private and the property of the parish. Records are to be kept in a locked file accessible only by the pastor and his delegate, the catechetical leader. A catechist may not view or remove documents without prior permission from the pastor. This is to protect the privacy of the catechist and the integrity of parish records.

Summary: "They Explained to Him the Way of God More Adequately"

Meanwhile a Jew named Apollos, a native of Alexandria, came to Ephesus. He was a learned man, with a thorough knowledge of the Scriptures. He had been instructed in the way of the Lord, and he spoke with great fervor and taught about Jesus accurately, though he knew only the baptism of John. He began to speak boldly in the synagogue. When Priscilla and Aquila heard him, they invited him to their home and

explained to him the way of God more adequately.
(Acts 18:24–26, NIV)

When Apollos became a catechist, we are told that he came under the supervision of Prisca and Aquila, two of the church's earliest catechetical leaders! Together, they "explained to him the way of God more adequately," even though he was already considered to be a man of "thorough knowledge of the Scriptures." As a catechetical leader, it is your responsibility to supervise and evaluate those who have been entrusted to you as catechists: you owe it to them and to the church. Your supervision and evaluation efforts ensure that the learning environment in your faith-formation program is Christ-centered and that the formation being provided is of the highest quality. Your catechists are already talented and knowledgeable people; however, through your ongoing supervision and evaluation efforts, you will help them to know "the way of God more adequately."

Growing as a Catechetical Leader

How would you describe your style of supervision? Use the following descriptors to get started, or create a few of your own: absent, demanding, encouraging, intense, motivating, thoughtful. What goals do you wish to set for yourself to improve your style of supervision? Of the four-step supervision process—assess, give feedback, evaluate, follow through—which steps do you already practice? Which step requires more practice?

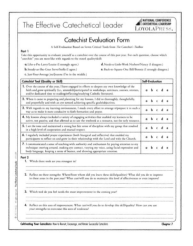

Go to www.loyolapress.com/ECL to access the worksheet.

Suggested Action

It's important for a catechist to get accustomed to the notion of being supervised. Tell your catechists at the next opportunity that they should get used to your presence in their learning space and that you will be conducting both informal and formal supervision and evaluation as the year goes on. The sooner catechists get used to seeing you walking around and dropping in on their classes, the less intimidated they will feel.

For Further Consideration

Shaping Spiritual Leaders: Supervision and Formation in Congregations. Abigail Johnson (Lanham, MD: Rowman & Littlefield Publishers, 2007).

Transforming the Rough Places: The Ministry of Supervision. Kenneth Pohly (Franklin, TN: Providence House Publishers, 2001).

2600 Phrases for Effective Performance Reviews. Paul Falcone (New York: AMACOM, 2005).

8

It's Rarely Simple: Handling Difficult Situations

Despite our best efforts, supervising human beings inevitably involves experiences of conflict. Catechetical leaders, like all those in ministry, are not exempt from this reality, and the process is rarely simple. The good news is that conflict, handled well, can be an opportunity for growth and that we can still function effectively as leaders in the midst of these human dynamics.

There's No Avoiding Conflict

Discord, in much of Christian thought, is understood as a consequence of sin: God intended for the world to live in harmony, but sin caused discord. As a result, Christians tend to see the presence of conflict in their communities as a sign of sin, a sign that something has gone terribly wrong and needs "fixing." Because conflict in this view is by definition a *chosen* evil—something we could have resisted but did not—it implies that some party must be to blame.

God created the world with a tremendous amount of diversity and, indeed, seems to glory in it. . . . Exposure to diversity, with its resulting experience of discomfort, surprise, and disagreement, appears to be the way that God matures creation. Tension seems to be built into the divine "development plan" as a means by which we grow into the kinds of people God dreams us to be. . . . People who can enjoy communion in diversity. (*Redeeming Conflict*, Ann M. Garrido, Ave Maria Press, 2016, 2–3)

For catechetical leaders, conflicts often present themselves at three distinct levels.

- Level 1: personal—conflicts between adult colleagues in ministry
- Level 2: professional—conflicts that require the catechetical leader to become involved
- Level 3: urgent—conflicts that must be addressed immediately and with the pastor

Level 1: Personal Conflict

Shaun came into my office visibly upset. "I can't believe what just happened! The youth-ministry leader asked me to help him create a new page for the parish Web site. He said it was important and urgent, so I worked all weekend to put it together—I even declined a movie invitation with friends on Saturday night so I could finish it. When I sent him the link on Monday, he said, 'Thanks, but the pastor and parish council decided to hold off on launching it until a later date.' I gave up my whole weekend for nothing! You're in charge—will you talk to the youth-ministry leader about this?"

In her book *Redeeming Conflict* on page 13, Ann Garrido describes this Level 1 scenario as a "triangulated relationship" with three roles to be played:

- the person who initiates the drawing in of a third party,
- the third party, and
- the absent party who is the topic of the conversation and presented in a negative light.

The initiator draws in a third party in an attempt to avoid having an uncomfortable conversation with the absent party. If you recognize an attempt to be drawn in as a third party, keep the following in mind:

- Listen with compassion.
- Insist that the initiator speak directly with the absent party.
- If necessary, offer to be present, but allow the initiator to lead the discussion and work toward resolution.

Level 2: Professional

> Tom noticed he had a phone message from a parent: "My daughter is in the second grade and preparing to receive first Holy Communion. I'm really upset by the way the catechist is teaching the children. All they do is read from a book and color. Sometimes the catechist is really late for class, so the children are waiting around and doing nothing. Not only is my daughter not learning anything, she's bored and doesn't want to go back to class! I voiced my concerns with the catechist, but nothing has changed."
>
> Tom sighed as he replayed the message. This was not the first complaint he had received about the catechist's teaching or absenteeism.

Because this issue calls into question the performance of the catechist and its possible effect on a student, it is classified as a professional issue, one that must be addressed by the catechetical leader. Here is a recommended path toward resolution.

- **Pray.** Call upon the gifts of the Holy Spirit—especially wisdom, understanding, counsel, knowledge, and fortitude—as you consider how best to approach the issue.
- **Discern.** Never act solely upon the opinion of one person. Perhaps you have already picked up on some performance trends.

If not, give the catechist the benefit of the doubt by spending time observing his or her performance for yourself.

- Make an appointment with your pastor to discuss your observations and your planned response. Handle the issue with respect and compassion for the catechist. Your goal is to correct the behavior, not to condemn.

- Make an appointment with the catechist and begin your session with prayer, keeping mindful of the continual presence of the Holy Spirit.

- Present the issue, and allow the catechist to tell his/her side of the story. Keep your remarks professional, not vague or judgmental, using language based on the observable. For example,

  ◦ Vague/judgmental statement: "A lot of parents are telling me lately that you're not doing a good job as a catechist. What's going on?"

  ◦ Professional statement based on the observable: "Over the past three weeks, two different parents voiced a concern about personal comments you've made about the Church in your lessons. Specifically, they tell me that you've shared that you see nothing wrong with couples living together and having children before marriage. Is this true? Let's discuss the issue."

  ◦ Vague/judgmental statement: "You don't seem to be ready to teach every week."

  ◦ Professional statement based on the observable: "It states in the handbook that catechists are required to arrive at least a few minutes before the start of class. This is to ensure that the children are properly supervised and that we are organized and ready to greet them and their parents warmly when they arrive. For the past three weeks, you have arrived at or after the start of class and without a prepared lesson. Let's discuss ways that you can get back on track."

- ○ Vague/judgmental statement: "You seem to be having trouble getting along with parents."
- ○ Professional statement based on the observable: "At the last two family gatherings, I noticed there was some tension between you and _____ when we discussed the retreat program. I will be speaking to _____ as well, but I was wondering if there was anything you wanted to share with me."

When to Redirect

We all hope for a positive outcome, one in which the catechist understands and makes the proper adjustments to behavior. There are times, however, when the catechist is either unable or unwilling to work toward resolution. If this happens, he or she must be redirected to another form of service. Instead of weekly duties as a primary catechist, perhaps the person may continue to contribute to the program through his or her gift of music, art, storytelling, or even administrative support.

Consider, too, consulting with your pastor regarding the stewardship plans for the parish. There are many forms of discipleship that put talents to good use and contribute to the common good. In the end, the person may not be pleased with the outcome. But in assessing the process, you and your pastor will know that you tried your best to emulate Jesus throughout the experience. Continue to be kind with each encounter. You will never regret taking the high road.

Level 3: Urgent

Sadly, there may arise the occasion when the immediate removal of a catechist is required, particularly when a student's health and/or safety is placed in jeopardy. Certain unethical, immoral, and illegal actions may also necessitate immediate action. Of course, it helps to have clear behavior expectations and consequences in your handbook for catechists!

If an allegation of unethical, immoral, or illegal behavior is reported to you, keep calm! Take a moment to pray for all those who are allegedly involved, then respond with a sense of urgency. Know and carefully follow the reporting procedures for your (arch)diocese. Always remember that in the case of alleged abuse of a minor, you are not an investigator and could cause the victim more harm than good if you place yourself in that role. We will deal in more depth in book 5 of this series with the difficult issue of removing a catechist from ministry.

A final and important point: Catechetical leaders play an important role in the prevention of the sexual abuse of minors. Be vigilant and pray often for the healing of victims of abuse.

Facing Inconvenient Truths

As a catechetical leader, you will sometimes need to face some inconvenient truths. Not every moment in faith formation can or should be warm and fuzzy. We sometimes need to address issues that are the cause of conflict in our communities. To do so is to take a prophetic and courageous stand in your ministry. To be prophetic, in biblical tradition, is to

- speak on behalf of the oppressed
- clearly and boldly speak God's Word
- bear witness
- bring hope to those in despair
- challenge people and institutions to be faithful
- fearlessly speak out about injustice.

The prophetic ministry—part of the threefold ministry of Christ as prophet, priest, and king—is something that we are all called to share in by virtue of our baptism. As a catechetical leader, you are sometimes called upon to practice this role in a more public manner than is typical of most Christians. In such cases it is critical that you contain your anger. In *7 Keys to Spiritual Wellness* on page 32, Joe Paprocki explains that too often our anger is expressed in such a way that

- it happens too quickly
- it is excessive
- its effects linger for too long.

He goes on to offer the following tips for how to handle situations when under pressure:

Stop. Take a few moments (count to ten) and breathe deeply. This can help you get your emotions in check.

Speak clearly. Once you've got your emotions in check and your thinking has been jump-started, express yourself without attacking the other person verbally. Clearly and assertively state your feelings and concerns.

Get active. Some kind of physical activity will stimulate various chemicals in the brain that can calm you down and help you to think more clearly.

Slow the game down. Consider your words carefully so that you don't say something you'll later regret. Slow down the "pace of the game" to allow cooler heads to prevail.

Seek a solution. Allow your thinking to move you from focusing on what has upset you to seeking a resolution.

Speak for yourself. Express yourself using "I" statements. Don't point fingers and throw fuel on the fire. Describe how you feel. Don't make accusations that begin with "you."

Use humor. Everyone involved will be able to think more clearly if the mood is lightened.

Use a lifeline! In some situations, we simply must admit that we aren't capable of thinking clearly. When this happens, invite another person to step in between you and the others involved, to help you all to think before acting.

Righteous Anger

Finally, it is important to remember that anger is not always a bad thing and is, in fact, at the heart of the prophetic mind-set of combating injustice. If we are not angry when we see people who are denied basic resources to sustain their human dignity, there is something wrong with us. In your role as a catechetical leader, you are at times called upon to respond to certain situations with righteous anger. But always keep in mind how God expresses anger in Scripture—not in a random and impulsive manner but in a way that is always directed at evil. Our God is passionate, and his anger is to be feared. However, the very people who often felt the brunt of God's anger, the Chosen People, were the same people who often described God as being "slow to anger."

None of us would be satisfied to have a passionless God who was indifferent to our comings and goings. In the same way, you will be called upon from time to time to show your passion. Be sure to do so in a way that leads people to conclude that when all is said and done, you are "slow to anger."

Summary: "First Be Reconciled to Your Brother"

"When you are offering your gift at the altar, if you remember that your brother or sister has something against you, leave your gift there before the altar and go; first be reconciled to your brother or sister, and then come and offer your gift." (Matt. 5:23–24)

Despite your best efforts as a catechetical leader, conflicts will arise and will need to be dealt with. It's part of the human condition. While we strive to avoid conflicts, we need to know how to deal with them when they surface. Conflicts come in all shapes and sizes: personal, professional, and urgent. In each case, it is important to respond to conflict in a manner befitting a disciple of Jesus Christ, which means that we are to deal with it in such a manner that justice and being "reconciled to your brother or sister" are seen as the ultimate goals. From time to time in your role, conflict will awaken your prophetic voice—that voice that is needed to speak out passionately about injustice. In doing so, you may find yourself moved to anger. Be cautious, and take steps to temper your anger and to express it, if unavoidable, in a manner that brings about the possibility of transformation and reconciliation.

Growing as a Catechetical Leader

Think about the experiences you have had handling conflict. Which experiences did you handle well, and what strategies can you glean from those moments? Which experiences do you feel you could have handled better, and what steps will you take to ensure that you are better prepared?

Go to www.loyolapress.com/ECL to access the worksheet.

Suggested Action

Some people come into ministry thinking that it will be free of the conflicts people experience in the "real world." This unrealistic expectation can lead people in ministry to be unprepared for the inevitable conflicts that arise in a group composed of diverse and imperfect human beings. Be a realist, and prepare yourself to deal with differences in a manner that befits a disciple of Christ. Begin by acknowledging to your catechists that conflict is a normal part of life in the church and that it will be dealt with appropriately.

For Further Consideration

Collaboration: Uniting Our Gifts in Ministry. Loughlan Sofield and Carroll Juliano (Notre Dame, IN: Ave Maria Press, 2000).

The Leadership Book. Charles J. Keating (Mahwah, NJ: Paulist Press, 1977).

Redeeming Conflict: 12 Habits for Christian Leaders. Ann M. Garrido (Notre Dame, IN: Ave Maria Press, 2016).

When Ministry Is Messy. Richard C. Brown (Cincinnati, OH: Franciscan Media, 2006).

9

Retaining Catechists: Support, Collaboration, Affirmation, and Public Recognition

Most catechists are not paid for their ministry. Thus, it is up to the catechetical leader to provide alternate ways of affirming catechists for the work they do. There are effective strategies for the catechetical leader to communicate support and affirmation for catechists, as well as ways to raise the role of the catechist through public recognition.

Everyone Loves Disneyland! (Right?)

When my daughter Kaimana was about five years old, my husband and I took her on her first trip to Disneyland. My sister and her family came along, including their two young children who were close in age and practically siblings to Kaimana. We all were excited to share this experience as a family and introduce her to the "Magic Kingdom." I recall thinking that this would be a day that she would remember for years to come.

It was, but not for the reason we expected.

As we entered the theme park, Kaimana was filled with anticipation. After all, back at home she enjoyed watching Disney animated movies, singing Disney songs, and holding her pink Minnie Mouse stuffed animal. She told me that she couldn't wait to go on all the rides and see her favorite characters.

But about two hours into our adventure I discovered two things about my daughter: 1) The sight of adults parading around in larger-than-life costumes frightened her; and 2) she preferred to cover her eyes at any display of bursting bright colors and cover her ears to loud music. How she managed to see or hear anything at the park that day remains a mystery to me. And then it started to rain. Not a gentle sprinkle but a torrential rain uncharacteristic of Southern California in the summer months.

Despite our cajoling, Kaimana, now an adult, has yet to make a return trip to Disneyland. We always laugh at her good-natured recollection: "I liked being with my family. But the Magic Kingdom was not what I expected and my socks got soaking wet."

Everyone Loves Being a Catechist! (Right?)

More than likely, as a catechetical leader, you have great enthusiasm for your ministry and expect that others have the same. "How could anyone *not* love being a catechist?" you ask. Each year you pray that most, if not all, of your catechists will enthusiastically sign up for another year and not walk away because their experience "was not what they expected" or their spirits felt "soaking wet"!

Granted, the Disneyland story is a whimsical way of introducing the challenges of retaining catechists. But there is a lesson to be learned: while Kaimana's assessment of her Disneyland experience as a five-year-old became a fun family legend, the fact is, while everyone else she was with has revisited the park, she has never returned. Catechetical leaders have the much nobler mission, given to us by Christ, of inviting and retaining catechists to bring forth not a magical kingdom but his "heavenly kingdom."

If you do experience either a high rate of turnover or reluctance among your best catechists to return for another year, take heart, for there is still hope! Let's take a few steps back to examine some of the basic principles and strategies for retention.

Intrinsic Motivation

What motivates us? A person who is intrinsically motivated engages in behavior because it is personally rewarding, not because he or she seeks recognition or external reward. There are several intrinsically motivated reasons that catechists share their gifts of faith and leadership skills with the church. Certainly, they believe that God has called them to assist the pastor with accompanying children and their parents on their journey of faith. Maybe their personal experience with raising their own children in faith motivates them to assist other families with strengthening the domestic church. Perhaps they desire to be part of something greater than themselves, to make a difference in the Church and in the lives of the people they serve.

Most of us can relate to these personal motives. Yet it's important to remember that the stirring in our hearts to serve the people of God does not originate within ourselves—it is given to us by God in the form of his grace. The *Catechism of the Catholic Church* teaches that

> Grace is first and foremost the gift of the Spirit who justifies and sanctifies us. But grace also includes the gifts that the Spirit grants us to associate us with his work, to enable us to collaborate in the salvation of others and in the growth of the Body of Christ, the Church. There are *sacramental graces*, gifts proper to the different sacraments. There are furthermore *special graces*, also called *charisms* after the Greek term used by St. Paul and meaning "favor," "gratuitous gift," "benefit." Whatever their character—sometimes it is extraordinary, such as the gift of miracles or of tongues—charisms are oriented toward sanctifying grace and are intended for the common good of the Church. They are at the service of charity which builds up the Church. (*CCC*, #2003)

Extrinsic Motivation

While intrinsically motivated responses to God's grace-filled prompt-ings are blessings to the church, there also are behaviors that are extrinsically motivated—that is, participating in an action for external rewards. If you're a paid employee, your wage is an external reward. Dutifully submitting the safe-environment audit information to the diocesan office in a timely manner, and thereby (joyfully) not receiving a reminder notice, is also a form of external reward. Offering extrinsic motivation can sometimes be helpful for motivating catechists.

- An external reward, such as providing a meal and childcare during catechist meetings, can increase participation.
- Publicly presenting certificates of completion whenever a catechist completes diocesan catechetical-certification requirements can motivate other catechists to complete their certification.
- Providing feedback can reinforce good or discourage poor performance.

It's a Balancing Act

The church is blessed by many intrinsically motivated catechists. That fact doesn't mean external rewards are not appreciated from time to time, especially expressed in the various forms of gratitude. This brightens up everyone's day! Two veteran catechetical leaders share their stories.

Story 1

Each year we serve approximately 150 families in our program. Par-ticipating in Catechetical Sunday is a great way to support, affirm, and recognize catechists. At my parish all catechists attend the Cat-echetical Sunday Mass. Prayer intentions are offered on their behalf, and they are called forward by our pastor to be blessed and commissioned to live out their calling. It's so meaningful to officially mark the beginning of the catechetical year with Eucharist. After all, our ministry is all about giving witness to Jesus by the way we live our lives, celebrate our faith, and share it with others.

We live in the state of Hawaii, so I like to present my catechists with a kukui nut lei at the Catechetical Sunday Mass. The kukui nut has a high oil content. In ancient Hawaii the oil was used as fuel for candles and torches—a critical source of light. Wearing the lei helps to remind catechists that they are called to be a light of Christ.

Catechists have always appreciated that we have a master calendar to follow throughout the religious-education year. They take part in the consultation process when selecting textbooks and other resources, so there is a sense of collaboration and empowerment. Once they receive their textbooks, I provide them with the support and guidance they need to prepare their lessons, especially for those who have no teaching experience. The catechists also appreciate that the children are happy with the program, because they are given opportunities to experience and live out their faith in the program and in the parish.

We have potluck gatherings at the beginning and end of the school year, which is a great way to build community. At a recent potluck I asked the children to surprise their catechist with a flower lei or a written note of thanks. It was really touching when these were presented to their catechists. I plan to do this annually!

I stay in contact with the catechists throughout the year, giving feedback and always, always thanking them. I use social media with the adult catechists to keep them informed of what's happening in the parish and program.

We have scheduled meetings, with snacks, prior to religious-education classes. At the end of the year we evaluate ourselves and the program, identifying the areas we can improve upon and what we did well and should continue to do.

Recognition is critically important for retention. Our religious-education program includes a 15-minute gathering of children and their parents at the beginning of each class. After Father leads us in prayer, I call on each class to come forward and announce the name of their catechist. This is a great way to make them known to parents and to the rest of the children in the program.

Once a month we offer a family faith-formation session. Parents enjoy meditating on Scripture, praying, and sharing their faith stories with one another, and supporting one another through the challenges of raising children in the faith. Many of these parents end up volunteering to assist catechists, which, again, leads to greater retention. And if I do need new catechists, I have a group of parents who already are involved in our ministry so are more willing to volunteer.

Story 2

I love my parish! In our religious-education program, we are blessed with over 120 volunteer catechists, aides, and staff. Each year we serve about five hundred children and youth, so our ministry is always buzzing, and it can be overwhelming. However, while responsibility for the program has been delegated to me by my pastor, I realized very early on that teamwork was vital in order to serve our families well. The camaraderie of the teams also helps with retention and minimizes burnout.

To retain catechists, first and foremost, make them feel welcome and important. Listen carefully to their input and allow them to implement ideas (taking care that they align with Church teachings). Mentor them into leadership positions. For example, once they are familiar with a retreat program, invite them to lead segments or to give testimony. They may be reluctant at first, but once they allow the Holy Spirit to move through them, they will discover a gift that they never knew they possessed. Mature teens and young adults, in particular, are astonished by the way God can work through them. It's marvelous to witness their development.

Retention is also high when entire families serve in ministry together—such as when a parent assists a lead catechist in the classroom. The grace there is that the lessons are being prepared and discussed in the home and maybe even during the commute to school/work during the week. The whole family grows in faith while serving!

When forming teams, it helps to remember that God has given each of us gifts and a generous spirit to share them. For example, not only are some of our catechists professional teachers, but several of them are trained to teach children with special learning needs. They become a very special team, providing a ministry that really touches the heart of the families they serve. A parent once said to me, "You know, I continually struggle with all the demands of providing an excellent (school) education for my child; I struggle with maneuvering through the medical insurance system so that my child can receive good medical care. Here at my parish is the one place where I feel supported and do not have to struggle. I am so grateful for the help I'm receiving to help my child come to know God and to be prepared for the sacraments."

Teams also include mentors for each grade level, those who enjoy organizing special programs, parish activities, and retreats, and—very important—those who enjoy hospitality, especially preparing and serving food.

When it comes to retention, it's important to have an open-door policy with understanding, compassion, and great love for one another. This takes a lot of energy. I pay close attention to my prayer life and my physical well-being, because these affect my administrative style and general attitude. I receive Eucharist frequently, commit to daily prayer, and make sure I allow myself to get the proper rest, nutrition, and exercise I need.

The Four Principles of Retention

A stool properly built on four legs is sturdy and reliable. Having a retention strategy using the four principles of retention—support, collaboration, affirmation, and public recognition—will go a long way in keeping your roll call of catechists sturdy and reliable. The two featured catechetical leaders clearly enliven the four principles, and because of it, they unleash one of the most powerful retention (and recruitment) tools available: personal testimony from the catechists themselves—also known as word of mouth. Catechists' desire to return for another year will increase when they are enthusiastic about their ministry and the way they are being treated. They not only return but they also often recruit others, especially their spouse, teen/young-adult child, or friend.

Here are more practical action steps to help bring the four principles of retention to life.

Support

- Match people to their abilities, not to your needs, allowing catechists to feel they're contributing according to their gifts. Some are more comfortable with little ones, some with adults, and others may enjoy adolescents or teens. Provide the resources necessary that "speak" to their learners in age-appropriate ways.

- Ask a parent to form a core prayer group to organize a prayer chain for your catechists and the children. Each week a family or parishioner will commit to pray for the catechists, the children, and their families. Prayer is always essential, particularly for those preparing to receive the sacraments.

- Provide a mentor for your catechists. This is especially important for young-adult catechists or those who have less than a year or two of experience.

- Speak with your pastor to discuss the priority issues of the catechetical program, and request that these issues be reflected in the overall parish pastoral plan. Resource allocation aligns with these very public priorities. These may include

  - Providing adequate teaching resources
  - Providing catechist-retreat resources

- ◦ Financing professional-development opportunities that take place out of state/region.

- Know the needs of your catechists, and provide workshops to help them grow in their ministry. For example, we discovered that several catechists had an interest in holding sacramental preparation sessions for children with special needs. We provided training for this, and we are now able to serve more of God's children.

- With the pastor, create a family atmosphere by greeting catechists warmly—be happy to see them! Provide regular feedback, and thank them often.

- When classes are in session, make yourself available to deal with major student-behavior issues should they arise. This frees catechists to focus on teaching, which they really appreciate.

Collaborate

- Get to know the catechetical leaders from your neighboring parishes. Plan a combined retreat for young people (perhaps prior to confirmation or receiving first Holy Communion) or for entire families. Collaborating connects us to the greater Christian community, distributes the workload, and allows catechists to serve and pray side by side.

- Form catechist teams in grade-level clusters (such as pre- and regular kindergarten, grades 1 and 2, grades 3 and 4, etc.). Provide opportunities for them to discuss and plan lessons together. Not only is it more enjoyable, but also there will be greater consistency across the grade levels.

- Invite mature teens to be classroom aides.

- If you share classroom space with the parish Catholic school, arrange for the teacher and catechist who share a classroom to meet and pray with each other. Have students write notes of prayer and thanksgiving to each other. Inspire them to realize that the Holy Spirit is truly alive, moving within the classroom walls and through each of them.

- Encourage catechists to participate in parish events, helping them to connect with parishioners who are not involved in the catechetical program.

Affirm

- Establish a volunteer "hierarchy" in which a catechist has an opportunity to advance over time. Each level allows for more self-direction and responsibility, which makes it feel like a "promotiopnn." Examples of catechist levels: Assistant, Lead, Mentor, grade-level or grade-cluster Coordinator.

- During the Easter season hold a prayer service for your catechists with a theme of affirmation. Provide a candle to each. Let them walk around the room saying a word/phrase of affirmation to their fellow catechists. This can be a powerful and bonding experience.

- Hold the affirmation prayer service with parents. Catechists and parents will have an opportunity to affirm each other.

- Work with your pastor to schedule his visits to the classrooms or at special events. Catechists know that pastors have busy schedules and appreciate their presence.

- On your catechist's baptism anniversary (or birthday), have students write notes of appreciation to their catechist.

- When you hold meetings, provide a light meal or snack and beverage. Thoughtful hospitality shows your catechists that you appreciate them.

- Hold "Coffee with Your Pastor" sessions with parents. During those sessions you will hear about the ways your catechists make a difference in the lives of the children. Sharing those stories with the catechists is a very affirming experience.

- Organize a celebratory gathering once or twice a year.

Give Public Recognition

- Celebrate Catechetical Sunday, traditionally celebrated on the third Sunday in September—a day on which parishes publicly recognize, pray for, and commission catechists before the assembly using the excellent resources provided by the USCCB. Parents are also recognized for their important role in forming their children in faith. While recognizing catechists within the community is important, highlight their spirit of volunteerism to the greater community as well. Catechetical Sunday resources are available at www.usccb.org.

- Regularly include program highlights in the diocesan newspaper or, when appropriate, in the secular newspaper. Share your stories to demonstrate how the students and their families are engaged in the life of the parish through the catechetical program.

- Feature captioned photos on the parish Web site, Facebook page, or Twitter account—be sure an image-release statement is included in your handbook and signed by anyone who is the subject of a photograph.

Summary: "We Always Thank God for You"

"We always thank God, the Father of our Lord Jesus Christ, when we pray for you, because we have heard of your faith in Christ Jesus and of the love you have for all God's people—the faith and love that spring from the hope stored up for you in heaven and about which you have already heard in the true message of the gospel that has come to you." (Col. 1:3–6, NIV)

St. Paul is consistent about many things, not the least of which is the fact that in every one of his letters in Scripture, he gives thanks to those who proclaim the word of God. Saint Paul knew that it was important to affirm his catechists for making a profound difference. And the catechists who stay year after year are the ones who feel they have made a significant difference.

Catechists believe they are called by God to serve. Many are intrinsically motivated to share their gifts in catechetical ministry. But retaining this precious human resource requires balancing what is expected of the catechist with what the catechist can expect from you. By reading the stories of veteran catechists and considering ways to implement the four principles of retention, it's clear that the pastor and catechetical leader wield the greatest influence for retention.

Does it take a great deal of effort and planning to support, form collaborative relationships with, affirm, and recognize your catechists? Yes! But it's worth the investment. When catechists feel their spirits come alive and see how their lives are enhanced as a volunteer in your program, your retention rates will soar.

Growing as a Catechetical Leader

When it comes to offering affirmation to others, the Golden Rule really applies: "Do unto others as you would have them do unto you." What kind of affirmation do you receive and appreciate most? How can you, in turn, most effectively express affirmation to your catechists for the service they provide?

Go to www.loyolapress.com/ECL to access the worksheet.

Suggested Action

In the coming week, make an effort to affirm and express thanks to as many people in your catechetical program as possible.

For Further Consideration

A Servant's Heart: 180 Encouraging Thoughts for Church Volunteers. Tiffany Ross (goTandem, 2015).

Servant Leadership Models for Your Parish. Dan Ebener (Mahwah, NJ: Paulist Press, 2010).

Shaping Spiritual Leaders: Supervision and Formation in Congregations. Abigail Johnson (Lanham, MD: Rowman & Littlefield Publishers, 2007).

10

No One Is an Island: Building and Nurturing a Catechetical Community

Every catechetical leader knows that it takes a lot of energy to recruit and retain catechists. It also takes a lot of energy to fashion them into a cohesive catechetical community. There is certainly no shortage of community-building ideas and activities. In fact, coaching a group of individuals to work together more effectively toward common goals is a multimillion-dollar industry bursting with activities designed to improve communication, problem solving, decision making, and so on.

So why not adopt some of these practices for our catechetical community and be done with it? Because we first need to ask ourselves *why* we're doing all of this! Recalling the principles discussed in chapter 6, we strive to expand our focus on "doing" community activities to "being" a community: the Body of Christ.

We Are the Body of Christ

When we build and nurture our community of catechists, what we really are doing is building and nurturing the Body of Christ. As we strengthen the Body, we enliven the words that Jesus taught us to pray: "Our Father in heaven, hallowed be your name. Your kingdom come. Your will be done, on earth as it is in heaven" (Matt. 6:9–10).

Jesus personally invited and formed a diverse group of twelve disciples into a community of faith. He taught them and sent them forth as his apostles to share the joy of the gospel, our message of salvation, to all peoples of the world. And so it is with our catechists, also a group of diverse individuals, whose vocation (calling) by Christ has brought them together to share the joy of the gospel. This is what Saint Paul speaks of in Ephesians:

> The gifts he gave were that some would be apostles, some prophets, some evangelists, some pastors and teachers, to equip the saints for the work of ministry, for building up the body of Christ, until all of us come to the unity of the faith and of the knowledge of the Son of God, to maturity, to the measure of the full stature of Christ. We must no longer be children, tossed to and fro and blown about by every wind of doctrine, by people's trickery, by their craftiness in deceitful scheming. But speaking the truth in love, we must grow up

in every way into him who is the head, into Christ, from whom the whole body, joined and knit together by every ligament with which it is equipped, as each part is working properly, promotes the body's growth in building itself up in love. (Eph. 4:11–16)

As with the human body, our catechetical community, while diverse, is healthiest when it functions as a whole. The Holy Spirit, who unites us in love, perfects us even in our weakness. In fact, sanctified by Christ, our imperfections can serve to strengthen the community.

> It is therefore of supreme importance that we consent to live not for ourselves but for others. When we do this we will be able first of all to face and accept our own limitations. . . . If we live for others, we will gradually discover that no one expects us to be "as gods." We will see that we are human, like everyone else, that we all have weaknesses and deficiencies, and that these limitations of ours play a most important part in all our lives. It is because of them that we need others and others need us. We are not all weak in the same spots, and so we supplement and complete one another, each one making up in himself for the lack in another. (Thomas Merton, *No Man Is an Island* [Chicago: Shambhala, 2005], xxi.)

What, then, does it take to build and nurture the catechetical community? Hopefully we realize that we are not attempting to cultivate a group of perfectly functioning individuals. Rather, it requires a focus on "being community," nurturing one another through our imperfections. We will explore this idea further through a series of community-building reflections.

Community as Sacred Interdependence

The classic Frank Sinatra tune "My Way" speaks to the importance we place on personal freedom and independence. But sometimes this can lead to loneliness. It's hard when we lose our connection to others or forget how good it feels to be able to rely on others and have others rely on us. A nurturing community is composed of this sacred interdependence that can have profound effects on people.

> I was a young mother and volunteer catechist when I was diagnosed with breast cancer. After each surgical procedure, family and friends were kind, always telling me to "call if you need anything." Feeling overwhelmed and facing an uncertain future, I never called anyone, relying solely on my immediate family. I insisted on driving myself to work, to medical appointments, and even radiation sessions—I just wanted to be alone with my thoughts, prayers, fears, and hopes.
>
> Midway through my treatment, my oncologist, who was kind but straightforward, asked, "Who are you allowing to help you through this?" I rattled off a short list of family members to which he replied, "What happened to your friends?" I looked him straight in the eye for a moment, then burst into tears.
>
> He placed a hand on my shoulder and said, "Look, your family has been great, but enjoying the company of friends can help in the process of healing and recovery. When you feel ready, it's okay to let your friends in. Let them treat you to a cup of tea and conversation. Accept a few invitations. Go for a walk, sing karaoke, or whatever interests you."
>
> Over time I felt God's hand weaving this single thread of a person back into the community. My catechist friends made it their mission to surround me with love. Reconnecting with others helped bring me out of my isolation and into communities of people I trusted. Here I was allowed to share my feelings, find comfort in regular social interaction, and worship and pray together.
>
> Whereas my focus was to survive, my community of family and friends nurtured within me a vibrant joy for life!

The Spirit of community experienced by this catechist is indeed sacred. In fact, the U.S. bishops teach us that

> the model for the human community is the Holy Trinity: the unity of Father, Son, and Holy Spirit. The very nature of the Trinity is communal and social. "God reveals himself to us as one who is not

alone, but rather as one who is relational, one who is Trinity. Therefore, we who are made in God's image share this communal, social
nature. We are called to reach out and to build relationships of love
and justice." The relationships that men and women are to establish
among themselves resemble the relationships between and among
the divine persons within the Triune God. Those human relationships transcend the boundaries of language, race, ethnicity, gender,
culture, and nation to bind people together in one human family.
Every single member of that one human family is of inestimable
worth, since each is made in the image of God and was created to
be happy with God for all eternity. (*NDC*, #43)

Seven Characteristics of a Nurturing Catechetical Community

Inspired by the words from our bishops and sacred Scripture, reflect
upon these seven characteristics of a nurturing community: mission,
joy, parameters, empowerment, recognition, engagement, and
stewardship.

1. **Mission.** I am grounded in our Roman Catholic faith and pray
   often with my colleagues so as to support one another in our
   mission to "Go into all the world and preach the gospel to all
   creation" (Mark 16:15, NIV).

2. **Joy.** A spirit of joy is evident in my interactions. "My soul
   magnifies the Lord" (Luke 1:46).

3. **Parameters.** I have a clear understanding of responsibilities and
   behavior expectations both for myself and from those in
   positions of leadership.

4. **Empowerment.** I pursue training and ongoing formation
   opportunities and am provided adequate resources for
   catechetical ministry. I realize that Christ himself has empowered
   me for mission since my baptism. I am grounded in prayer and
   participate frequently in the sacraments of reconciliation and

Eucharist so as to attune my heart to Christ. "The good person out of the good treasure of the heart produces good, and the evil person out of evil treasure produces evil; for it is out of the abundance of the heart that the mouth speaks" (Luke 6:45).

5. **Recognition.** I receive recognition in many forms, such as commissioning, public recognition, verbal thanks, special gatherings, a ministry badge, etc.

6. **Engagement.** I participate in parish-wide events and share the light of faith with the greater community through personal and professional networks, political involvement, etc.

7. **Stewardship.** I embrace catechesis as a way of life and seek ways to make a difference by connecting faith and life in contemporary culture. "I must proclaim the good news of the kingdom of God to the other cities also; for I was sent for this purpose" (Luke 4:43).

For Reflection and Discussion: In what ways are you living out these characteristics of a nurturing community?

The Growing Pains of Community

I once asked a religious Brother, who is a good friend of mine, to name a favorite aspect of community. His enthusiastic response: "My Brothers!" When asked to name a challenging aspect of community, with a twinkle in his eye he responded, "My Brothers!" And so it is with building community. Though we continually strive for Christian unity, the Body of Christ, as with the human body, experiences aches and growing pains from time to time. Take heart—by recognizing symptoms of pain and responding to the root cause, the community can be nurtured back to health.

A catechetical leader reflects on the lessons she learned on her journey from injury to healing:

The first twinge of pain came in my shoulder area. I rated it a 4 on a scale of 1 to 10 and shrugged it off as spending too much time in front of my computer. After all, our parish would soon begin the immediate preparation process for first Holy Communion, and there were parent letters, certificates, bulletin announcements, and parent/catechist reminders to issue. I bought an ergonomic chair in an attempt to improve my posture and alleviate the pain.

Several weeks later, a constant throb developed in my right elbow, so I wrapped it tightly in an Ace bandage, attempting to ease the pain by managing my movements. I remember having to use my left hand to distribute an unconsecrated host as I prepared each child to reverently receive the body of Christ.

A few days after that, sharp pain in my right hand jolted me awake in the middle of the night. Reaching over to the lamp on my nightstand, I realized with horror that my fingers were so numb with pain that I could barely flip on the light switch. I thought I was having a heart attack! An urgent visit to the hospital and several scans later revealed the source of my trauma: a herniated disc in my cervical (neck) region.

Then came the treatment: prescription medication to ease the pain, followed by physical therapy and visits to a chiropractor. Throughout each phase, I found it interesting that no one on my medical team paid much attention to my shoulder, elbow or hand—the pain in those areas was declared merely symptomatic of the root cause. Thus, my attempts to heal myself through ergonomics and Ace-bandaging were futile, because I really didn't understand what was happening within my body.

What I experienced with my physical body can be related to the Body of Christ, particularly my community of catechists. If symptoms start to develop, I try to identify the source of pain to facilitate the healing process.

Symptoms in Ourselves

We may become aware of our own symptoms, such as fatigue, distract-edness, or a diminishing prayer life. It's important to practice self-care. Here are some ways we can do this.

- Praying. Prayer techniques such as the Daily Examen, developed by Saint Ignatius of Loyola, allow us to reflect on the events of the day, detect God's presence, and discern his direction for our lives.
- Being mindful of the gifts of sanctifying grace received in baptism. These gifts enable us to "believe in God—to hope in him, and to love him through the theological virtues" and give us "the power to live and act under the prompting of the Holy Spirit through the gifts of the Holy Spirit" (*CCC*, #1266).
- Maintaining a healthy lifestyle (getting enough sleep, exercise, and a proper nutritious diet).
- Reaching out to others for support.

Symptoms in Our Community

Sometimes symptoms of weakness in the body arise in our community, such as frequent absenteeism, interpersonal tensions, and repeated use of divisive "us versus them" statements (e.g., "Those parents never bring their children to church," "Those children should take their lessons more seriously," "Those parishioners don't appreciate us.") Nurture the community by

- speaking confidentially with each individual in a spirit of joy and compassion.
- listening and responding to their needs to the best of your ability.
- praying together as a community.

The Evangelizing Community

Whether you're a first-year or veteran catechetical leader, you realize that balancing the operational aspects of the program and the pastoral care of the catechists is not only complex, but it's downright messy work! With the amount of energy it takes to run the program, it can be easy to focus our evangelizing efforts only upon the children who are registered in our program. But we also need to stay attuned to the needs of their families and the greater community.

We can seize opportunities to share the joy of the gospel, our message of salvation, sometimes in the most unexpected ways, by being attentive to the many opportunities that God provides us. After all, God always is prompting us to participate in a love story that is unfolding right before our eyes. A catechetical leader shares her story:

> One Saturday morning I was conducting my monthly catechist meeting. I was just about to begin a lesson-planning session when we heard a soft knock at the door. Standing at the entrance was a young couple, looking a bit perplexed. "We're looking for the pastor."
>
> "I believe he's in the rectory. Is there something that I can help you with?"
>
> Removing a small container from his backpack, the young man softly replied, "Father said that he would bless our baby. My wife was twelve weeks pregnant when she had a miscarriage. I guess this is our baby's funeral." He continued, "We were raised Catholic, and as kids we even went to religious-education classes. Over time we just stopped going to Mass. But when we were at the hospital after the miscarriage, we found ourselves surrounded by people who were praying for us. The hospital asked if we wanted the 'fetal tissue.' It was shocking to hear them refer to our son or daughter in that way. We said, 'We don't want fetal tissue. What we do want is our "baby."' Since then my wife and I have been saying the same prayers we learned as kids, and that made us realize that God is always with

us. We knew that we needed to make our way back to the Church and to the people who prayed for and supported us, who share our values and understand how we feel."

By that time, all my catechists had surrounded this couple and had been brought to tears by their witness. We hugged them warmly, expressed our sorrow for their loss, and prayed over them for a few minutes. Leaving our lesson planning behind, one of the catechists headed to the rectory to notify the pastor while the rest of us accompanied the couple to the church. The service, although brief, was one of the most profound experiences of my life.

Afterward, I asked if they wanted to join me for a cup of coffee. They declined but did accept a Bible from me. Handing it to them, I said, "I'd like to read a psalm to you, Psalm 23:4. 'Even though I walk through the darkest valley, I fear no evil; for you are with me; your rod and your staff—they comfort me.' I pray over these words in times of struggle in my life. I hope that you will find comfort in them and throughout this holy book."

I called them later in the week to invite them to Mass. They've been attending faithfully ever since.

Oh, and my catechists had to finish their lesson plans on their own. When I looked over the plans, they were some of the best lessons the catechists had ever written.

A Field Hospital

In his 2016 book *The Name of God is Mercy,* Pope Francis offers this statement: "I like to use the image of a field hospital to describe this 'Church that goes forth' . . . toward those who are 'wounded,' who are in need of an attentive ear, understanding, attentiveness and love" (Pope Francis, *The Name of God is Mercy* [New York, NY: Random House, 2016] 80).

The young couple, spiritually wounded by the loss of their child, began to experience God's healing and comfort through the kindness of others. Woundedness, while perhaps not on this scale, touches everyone's lives—relationship struggles, separation, illness, loneliness, and so on. We know this through our own personal experiences and through the stories of the children and families we serve. We also know that God reveals himself in a special way, time and time again, in every compassionate response.

The Body of Christ exists not solely for the benefit of its own members. In fact, we are strengthened when we bring Christ's presence and healing beyond the walls of the classroom and into the lives of the families we serve and the greater community. Add to this list some of the ways your community has touched the lives of the families and greater community that you serve:

- the parents who had their marriage convalidated so they could receive first Holy Communion with their child
- a mother who entered the catechumenate along with her children
- the parents who volunteered to be catechists because they are inspired by their child's experience in the catechetical program
- parents who returned to the Church and are renewing their own practice of our faith after many years of being "too busy"
- the child who was reluctant to participate in class in her regular school but sang like an angel at the parish Christmas program, astonishing her family
- volunteers who coordinate fund-raising and school-supply drives to assist families in need

Sharing stories like these nurtures the catechetical community because they serve as reminders that through the power of the Holy Spirit, we are bearers of the gospel.

The Be-Attitudes of Community

An attitude is a settled way of thinking about someone or something. The good news is that we can find inspiration for community building by examining the wisdom and experiences of the Church.

The catechetical community grows stronger when, together, we intentionally engage in meaningful practices that are rooted in the teachings of the Church. For example, the *Catechism of the Catholic Church* teaches us that the Beatitudes (Matt. 5:1–10) are at the heart of Jesus' preaching because they fulfill God's promises made to the chosen people since Abraham. The Beatitudes are "be-attitudes" because they are ways of be-ing that help us to lead happy (blessed) lives and be rewarded in heaven.

> The Beatitudes depict the countenance [demeanor] of Jesus Christ and portray his charity. They express the vocation of the faithful associated with the glory of his Passion and Resurrection; they shed light on the actions and attitudes characteristic of the Christian life; they are the paradoxical promises that sustain hope in the midst of tribulations; they proclaim the blessings and rewards already secured, however dimly, for Christ's disciples; they have begun in the lives of the Virgin Mary and all the saints. (*CCC*, #1717)

Thoughtful reflection on the Beatitudes is a great way to build community. Human beings are social by nature, and the Beatitudes, which in many ways gave rise to Catholic social teaching, emphasize our Christian discipleship and take us into the deeper, more meaningful aspects of salvation. They move us beyond the operational aspects of the catechetical program to the mission of the Christian community.

And so, as we end this book, I invite you to consider how you, as a catechetical leader, are helping to build a Beatitude community—a community that strives to embody the vision of the kingdom of God that Jesus shared in his Sermon on the Mount.

Blessed are the poor in spirit, for theirs is the kingdom of
heaven.
Blessed are those who mourn, for they will be comforted.
Blessed are the meek, for they will inherit the earth.
Blessed are those who hunger and thirst for righteousness, for
they will be filled.
Blessed are the merciful, for they will receive mercy.
Blessed are the pure in heart, for they will see God.
Blessed are the peacemakers, for they will be called children
of God.
Blessed are those who are persecuted for righteousness' sake,
for theirs is the kingdom of heaven.
(Matt. 5:3–10)

Heavenly Father, you alone are the source of hope and new life in the midst of our weakness and suffering. Help us to be a community who is open to your grace and presence, trusting that we find complete fulfillment only when we orient our lives to you. As your grace unfolds in our lives, may we be agents of your grace to others, serving them well in your name, a vibrant faith-filled community worthy of your promise to "rejoice and be glad, for your reward is great in heaven" (Matt. 5:12, NIV).

We make this prayer through Jesus, our Lord. Amen.

Summary: "Its Many Parts Form One Body"

Just as a body, though one, has many parts, but all its many parts form one body, so it is with Christ. For we were all baptized by one Spirit so as to form one body—whether Jews or Gentiles, slave or free—and we were all given the one Spirit to drink. Even so the body is not made up of one part but of many. (1 Cor. 12:12–14)

Ultimately, the work of the church is to build the Body of Christ. Thus, building and nurturing relationships is at the core of ministry. Catechists benefit from the recognition that they belong to a unique catechetical community in which they can find support, encourage-ment, and inspiration. In your role as a catechetical leader, you are called to build a catechetical community that nurtures the vocation of the catechist within a community of believers that understands itself as being a catechizing community. As a community builder, your task is not about cultivating a group of perfectly functioning individuals but about nurturing one another through our imperfections.

Growing as a Catechetical Leader

Our community of faith exists for one purpose: to evangelize. Reflect upon the following papal quotes, and describe ways in which you and your community of catechists may live up to the challenges of evangelization stated by our Holy Fathers.

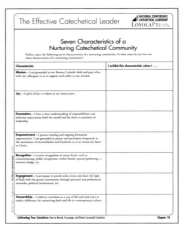

Modern man listens more willingly to witnesses than to teachers, and if he does listen to teachers, it is because they are witnesses.

—Pope Paul VI

Don't be afraid of the radicalness of His demands. . . . If He asks much of you, it is because He knows you can give much.

—Saint John Paul the Great

Tell others about the truth that sets you free.

—Pope Benedict XVI

We cannot keep ourselves shut up in parishes, in our communities, when so many people are waiting for the Gospel!

—Pope Francis

Go to www.loyolapress.com/ECL to access the worksheet.

Suggested Action

Read and reflect on these words of Pope Benedict XVI:

> By faith, the Apostles left everything to follow their Master (cf. Mk 10:28). . . . By faith, the disciples formed the first community. . . . By faith, the martyrs gave their lives. . . . By faith, men and women have consecrated their lives to Christ. . . . By faith, across the centuries, men and women of all ages, whose names are written in the Book of Life (cf. Rev. 7:9, 13:8), have confessed the beauty of following the Lord Jesus. . . . By faith, we too live: by the living recognition of the Lord Jesus, present in our lives and in our history. (Pope Benedict XVI, *Porta Fidei*, #13)

For Further Consideration

Building Community: Christian, Caring, Vital (Loughlan Sofield, Carroll Juliano, and Rosine Hammett, Ave Maria Press, 1998).

Building Strong Church Communities (Patricia Wittberg, SC, Paulist Press, 2012).

Evangelii Gaudium—The Joy of the Gospel (Pope Francis).

About the Author

Jayne Ragasa-Mondoy serves as Director of Religious Education for the Diocese of Honolulu, which is composed of the six major islands in the state of Hawaii. Her responsibilities include oversight of catechesis and evangelization programs and the formation of catechetical leaders. Born and raised in Honolulu, Jayne began her professional career in corporate management in the San Francisco Bay Area while remaining steadily involved in parish catechetical and liturgical music programs. Jayne, husband Timothy, and daughter Catherine returned to Honolulu, where Jayne earned a master's degree in pastoral leadership from Chaminade University of Honolulu. Her perspective of volunteer recruitment and management is shaped by her lengthy experience in working with and leading volunteers in diocesan and parish catechetical ministries, as a high school teacher and administrator, and as a board member for local Catholic and private schools and the National Conference for Catechetical Leaders (NCCL).

The Effective Catechetical Leader Series

Whether you are starting out as a catechetical leader or have been serving as one for many years, **The Effective Catechetical Leader** series will help you use every aspect of this ministry to proclaim the Gospel and invite people to discipleship.

Called by Name
Preparing Yourself for the Vocation of Catechetical Leader

Catechetical Leadership
What It Should Look Like, How It Should Work, and Whom It Should Serve

Developing Disciples of Christ
Understanding the Critical Relationship between Catechesis and Evangelization

Cultivating Your Catechists
How to Recruit, Encourage, and Retain Successful Catechists

Excellence in Ministry
Best Practices for Successful Catechetical Leadership

All God's People
Effective Catechesis in a Diverse Church

Each book in **The Effective Catechetical Leader** series is available for $13.95, or the entire series is available for $65.00.

To Order:
Call **800.621.1008** or visit **loyolapress.com/ECL**

The ECL App

Everything You Need to Be an Effective Catechetical Leader

The ECL app puts wisdom and practical help at your fingertips. Drawn directly from the six books of **The Effective Catechetical Leader** series, ECL provides an opportunity for catechetical leaders to center themselves spiritually each day, focus on specific pastoral issues, and identify go-to strategies for meeting the challenges of serving as an effective catechetical leader.

Special Features:

- Over 40 unique guided reflections tailored to your individual pastoral ministry needs.
- On-the-go convenience and accessibility on your phone or tablet.
- Modern design, easy-to-use interface, and a source of calm amidst the busy schedule of a catechetical leader.

For more details and to download the app, visit
www.loyolapress.com/ECL